# THE
# MONETARY
# SIN OF
# THE WEST

# Jacques Rueff

---

# THE
# MONETARY
# SIN OF
# THE WEST

Translated by Roger Glémet

---

THE MACMILLAN COMPANY

NEW YORK, NEW YORK

Copyright © 1972 by Jacques Rueff

© Librairie Plon, 1971

The Macmillan Company
866 Third Avenue, New York, N.Y. 10022
Collier-Macmillan Canada Ltd., Toronto, Ontario

*The Monetary Sin of the West* was originally published in French by Lib-rairie Plon under the title *Le Péché Monétaire de l'Occident* and is reprinted by permission.

Library of Congress Catalog Card Number: 79–182450

First Printing

Printed in the United States of America

There is tragedy in the world because
men contrive, out of nothings, tragedies
that are totally unnecessary—which means
that men are frivolous.

—Henry de Montherlant,
*La Rose de Sable*

# Contents

*Prologue*

# PROLOGUE

The problem of Western currency is more topical than ever. For ten years now, the international monetary system has been patched up by many expedients that were intended to extend its assured life. It cannot endure very long in the present state.

The following pages afford a description of its modifications over time. They provide a diagnosis and make a prognosis possible.

Some qualification is necessary, however, as regards the rate of foreseeable evolution. The art of monetary expedients has been refined to such a point over the last ten years that no one can predict what artificial devices can be generated by the fertile minds of experts. One thing is certain, however: while additional innovations may stave off the gradual deterioration of the system for a while, they cannot change the outcome. As far as prognostication is concerned, events can never be wrong. But unfortunately, events have already passed judgment. It is to be hoped that they will not continue to show that in the monetary field, as indeed in other fields, the same causes always bring about the same effects, and those who persist in ignoring the past are irrevocably doomed to live the same sequence of events again.

# PART ONE

# Introducing
# the Gold-Exchange
# Standard

# I

## THE DIAGNOSIS OF
## JUNE 1961

Some will no doubt be surprised that in 1961, practically alone in the world, I had the audacity to call attention to the dangers inherent in the international monetary system as it existed then.[1]

My fears at the time were based essentially on the growing similarities between the international monetary developments of the years 1958–1961 and those of the latter part of the 1926–1929 period. There was the same accumulation of Anglo-Saxon currencies in the monetary reserves of European countries, in particular France, and the same inflation in creditor countries.

In both periods the monetary system was characterized by the widespread application of a specific, adventitious procedure that Anglo-Saxon countries termed the gold-exchange standard.

What marks this system is that, *de jure* or *de facto,* in the coun-

[1] I must, however, pay a tribute here to my friend Professor Robert Triffin of Yale University, who also diagnosed the threat of the gold-exchange standard to the stability of the Western world. But while we agreed on the diagnosis, we differed widely as to the remedy to be applied. On the other hand, the late Professor Michael Heilperin, of the Graduate Institute of International Studies in Geneva, held a position in every respect close to mine.

tries it affects, the counterpart in the balance sheet of the bank of issue for the amount of money in circulation is not only gold or claims denominated in the national currency, as is the case under the gold standard. It also includes a large proportion of foreign currencies that are freely convertible into gold—that is to say, in the 1925–1930 period, dollars and sterling, and since 1945, dollars only.

The last section of this chapter (see pages 31–35) records in greater detail the main features of this system and provides some information relating to its origins and scope of application.

Between 1930 and 1934 I was Financial Attaché in the French Embassy in London. In that capacity, I had noted day after day the dramatic sequence of events that turned the 1929 cyclical downturn into the Great Depression of 1931–1934. I knew that this tragedy was due to disruption of the international monetary system as a result of requests for reimbursement in gold of the dollar and sterling balances that had been so inconsiderately accumulated.

On 1 October 1931 I wrote a note to the Finance Minister, in preparation for talks that were to take place between the French Prime Minister, whom I was to accompany to Washington, and the President of the United States. In it I called the Government's attention to the role played by the gold-exchange standard in the Great Depression, which was already causing havoc among Western nations, in the following terms:

> There is one innovation which has materially contributed to the difficulties that are besetting the world. That is the introduction by a great many European states, under the auspices of the Financial Committee of the League of Nations, of a monetary system called the gold-exchange standard. Under this system, central banks are authorized to include in their reserves not only gold and claims denominated in the national currency, but also foreign exchange. The latter, although entered as assets of the central bank which owns it, naturally remains deposited in the country of origin.

The use of such a mechanism has the considerable drawback of damping the effects of international capital movements in the financial markets that they affect. For example, funds flowing out of the United States into a country that applies the gold-exchange standard increase by a corresponding amount the money supply in the receiving market, without reducing in any way the money supply in their market of origin. The bank of issue to which they accrue, and which enters them in its reserves, leaves them on deposit in the New York market. There they can, as previously, provide backing for the granting of credit.

Thus the gold-exchange standard considerably reduces the sensitivity of spontaneous reactions that tend to limit or correct gold movements. For this reason, in the past the gold-exchange standard has been a source of serious monetary disturbances. It was probably one cause for the long duration of the substantial credit inflation that preceded the 1929 crisis in the United States. The first action of an international conference that was resolved seriously to deal with monetary problems should be to eliminate it.

On 17 March 1933, in a lecture given at the *Ecole des Sciences politiques* under the chairmanship of the Finance Minister, Mr. Pierre-Etienne Flandin, I expatiated in greater detail on the same considerations, as follows:

The gold-exchange standard is characterized by the fact that it enables the bank of issue to enter in its monetary reserves not only gold and paper in the national currency, but also claims denominated in foreign currencies, payable in gold and deposited in the country of origin. In other words, the central bank of a country that applies the gold-exchange standard can issue currency not only against gold and claims denominated in the national currency, but also against claims in dollars or sterling.

This recommendation did not remain a dead letter. It was followed systematically by the Financial Committee of the League of Nations, which introduced the system in all the countries where it was called upon to intervene: Austria, Hungary, Greece, Bulgaria, Estonia, Danzig. . . . In 1928, when France introduced its monetary reform, it refused to accept it *de jure*. Yet it did yield to Britain's request by including *de facto* in the Treasury assets dollars and pounds sterling—as against advances by the Bank of France, which was tantamount to including them indirectly in its monetary reserves.

The application of the gold-exchange standard had the considerable advantage for Britain of masking its real position for many years. During the entire postwar period, Britain was able to loan to Central European countries funds that kept flowing back to Britain, since the moment they had entered the economy of the borrowing countries, they were deposited again in London. Thus, like soldiers marching across the stage in a musical comedy, they could reemerge indefinitely and enable their owners to continue making loans abroad, while in fact the inflow of foreign exchange which in the past had made such loans possible had dried up.

On the other hand, in the monetary field, this system had considerable adverse effects. In the first instance, it substantially impaired the sensitivity and efficacy of the gold-standard mechanism. Funds flowing out of the United States into a gold-exchange-standard country, for instance, increase by a corresponding amount the money supply in the recipient market, while the money supply in the American market is not reduced. The bank of issue that receives the funds, while entering them directly or indirectly in its reserves, leaves them on deposit in the New York market. There thy contribute, as before being transferred, to the credit base.

But there is more. The gold-exchange standard dissociates credit movements from gold movements. For instance, in 1927 and 1928 it enabled large amounts of capital that had been exported to the United States and Britain to flow back to Continental Europe, without the bullion reserves of these countries being in any way affected. In this way it not only operated to loosen the link between credit and gold, it severed it altogether. Thus it contributed to prolonging and accentuating the abnormal distribution of gold, since the net result was that capital could flow back without any flowback of gold.

By the same token, the gold-exchange standard was a formidable inflation factor. Funds that flowed back to Europe remained available in the United States. They were purely and simply increased twofold, enabling the American market to buy in Europe without ceasing to do so in the United States. As a result, the gold-exchange standard was one of the major causes of the wave of speculation that culminated in the September 1929 crisis. It delayed the moment when the braking effect that would otherwise have been the result of the gold standard's coming into play would have been felt.[2]

The wiser for this experience, I witnessed with great concern, after the Second World War, the resurgence of the practices that had brought about the Great Depression after the First World War. However, their consequences had been masked until 1958 because they were hidden and given an inverse orientation by the process of inflation in individual countries that had generated the dollar shortage.

It was only after convertibility had been restored for the major

[2] The text of this lecture was published in *Les Doctrines monétaires à l'épreuve des faits* (Paris: Alcan, 1932) and in the *Revue des Deux Mondes*, 1932. The text of the lecture was also reproduced in full in *The Age of Inflation*, Eng. trans. (Chicago: Regnery, 1964), p. 30.

European currencies that the consequences of the gold-exchange standard became a dominant feature again.

As I observed, from then on, the development of a situation that was basically analogous to the events that had culminated in the 1931 catastrophe, I felt it my duty to do my utmost to ward off this gathering peril.

Availing myself of the authority I had derived from the successful outcome of the financial rehabilitation operation of December 1958, I first brought the matter to the attention of the Finance Minister, as was only logical. In a note dated 10 January 1959, quoted below (see pages 62–63), I called his attention to the modalities of the convertibility of the French national currency that had just been restored. I observed that in future, under the Bretton Woods agreements, francs would be convertible into dollars but the dollar alone would be convertible into gold. I was convinced, however, that convertibility of the dollar into gold had become precarious as a result of the widespread application of the gold-exchange standard. I therefore suggested that the Government consider the nature of the relationship of the dollar to gold and initiate the necessary steps with a view to reestablishing an international monetary system of a lasting nature.

My recommendations were not only criticized but violently assailed by the Finance Ministry. Yet I did not lose hope of securing from the Government some international action with a view to remedying a monetary system that, in view of everybody's failure to realize what was happening, seemed to me fraught with immense danger. I therefore resolved to warn public opinion of the perils to which order, stability, and economic prosperity in the West were being exposed.

I first sounded the alarm in three articles published in *Le Monde* on 27, 28, and 29 June 1961. These articles were widely read, since they were reproduced on the same dates in the London *Times,* the *Neue Züricher Zeitung,* the *Corriere della Sera, Orientation Economique* (Caracas), and in the American magazine *Fortune* for July 1961.

The text of the three articles published by *Le Monde* is reproduced here, with the subtitles inserted by the editor:

## THE GOLD-EXCHANGE STANDARD:
## A DANGER TO THE WEST

### I. THE NATURE OF THE EVIL

In all countries where the currency is connected with the dollar, the situation each day becomes more and more similar to that which turned the recession of 1929 into a Great Depression.

The instability of the monetary structure is such that the merest incident in international relations on the economical or financial plan would be enough to lead to world disaster.

Yet the remedies proposed during current negotiations will not get down to the root of the trouble, but instead will prolong for a few months or a few years the mistakes that have led to the present situation.

Indeed, for the West, the most urgent duty is to acknowledge the danger that threatens it, to ward it off, thereby reestablishing in the free world a monetary system that will generate equilibrium and endurance.

### *The Losers Get Their Stakes Back*

From 1926 to 1929, the world of monetary convertibility rode the crest of a wave of unprecedented expansion.

If one analyzes the components of the monetary situation at that time, one will see that it was characterized by a massive influx of capital, coming from England and the United States, first to Germany, as a consequence of the financial rehabilitation achieved by the Dawes plan (1924), and secondly France, after the Poincaré restoration operation (1926–1928).

But these transfers of capital were of an entirely new character and apparently very unusual. In fact, the liquid funds, although entering into the economy of the recipient countries—essentially

Germany and France, where they were generators of extra credit—
did not leave the countries of origin overseas.

This paradoxical situation was the effect of a profound modification, insidiously brought about, in the monetary systems of convertible-currency countries in pursuance of a recommendation by
the International Monetary Conference that met at Genoa in April–
May 1922.

Resolution 9 of this conference urged "the conclusion of an
international convention for savings in the use of gold by maintaining reserves in the form of foreign balances."

It is in the application of this recommendation that the conditions
known only under the Anglo-Saxon name of "gold-exchange standard" replaced the old gold standard after the First World War—
mainly in France and Germany and in all countries whose currencies had been restored by the Financial Committee of the League of
Nations.

Under this system, the banks of issue are authorized to create
money which is backed not only by claims denominated in the
national currency and by their gold stock, but also by foreign
exchange payable in gold—that is to say, after the First World War,
payable in pounds sterling and dollars.

As a result of this large influx of sterling and dollars from overseas to the countries that had recently recovered, the Continental
banks of issue did not ask for payment in gold, as they would have
been required to do, at least for the most part of those resources,
under the gold standard. Instead, they left the pounds and dollars
in deposit at their place of origin, where they were usually loaned
to national borrowers. The banks of issue viewed this new system
with all the more favor because it substituted in their balance sheets
interest-bearing assets for ingots or gold specie that were entirely
unproductive.

The unending feedback of the dollars and pounds received by
the European countries to the overseas countries from which they
had come reduced the international monetary system to a mere
child's game in which one party had agreed to return the loser's
stake after each game of marbles.

## The Secret of a Deficit Without Tears

To verify that the same situation exists in 1960, *mutatis mutandis,* one has only to read President Kennedy's message of 6 February 1961 on the stability of the dollar.

He indicates with admirable objectivity that from 1 January 1951 to 31 December 1960, the deficit of the balance of payments of the United States had attained a total of $18.1 billion.

One could have expected that during this period the gold reserve would have declined by the same amount. Amounting to $22.8 billion on 31 December 1950, it was, against all expectations, $17.5 billion on 31 December 1960.

The reason for this was simple. During this period the banks of issue of the creditor countries, while creating, as a counterpart to the dollars they acquired through the settlement of the American deficits, the national currency they remitted to the holders of claims on the United States, had reinvested about two-thirds of these same dollars in the American market. In doing so between 1951 and 1961 the banks of issue had increased by about $13 billion their foreign holdings in dollars.

Thus, the United States did not have to settle that part of their balance-of-payments deficit with other countries. Everything took place on the monetary plane just as if the deficit had not existed.

In this way, the gold-exchange standard brought about an immense revolution and produced the secret of a deficit without tears. It allowed the countries in possession of a currency benefiting from international prestige to give without taking, to lend without borrowing, and to acquire without paying.

The discovery of this secret profoundly modified the psychology of nations. It allowed countries lucky enough to have a boomerang currency to disregard the internal consequences that would have resulted from a balance-of-payments deficit under the gold standard.

The gold-exchange standard thus brought about conditions propitious to the major change that the donation policy has introduced into international tradition. Leaving to the donor country the joy of giving and to the beneficiary the joy of receiving, it had only one consequence: the monetary situation which President Kennedy outlined, and whose effects we now have to describe.

In attempting to describe those consequences I shall certainly not lose sight of the fact that the U.S. balance-of-payments deficits over the past decade have been outweighed by the grants and loans they accorded with unprecedented generosity to nations that experienced a foreign exchange shortage after the war.

But the method of giving is no less important than the object of the gift itself, in particular when it is likely seriously to affect stability and the very existence of the receiving and donor countries alike.

In addition, the situation I am going to analyze was neither brought about nor specifically wanted by the United States. It was the outcome of an unbelievable collective mistake which, when people become aware of it, will be viewed by history as an object of astonishment and scandal.

## 2. Two Pyramids of Credit Built on the U.S. Gold Stock

The substitution of the gold-exchange standard for the gold standard entails three essential consequences:

First, under the gold standard, any balance-of-payments deficit had the effect of restricting purchasing power in the deficit country, as a result of the settlement that gave rise to a transfer.

Under the gold-exchange standard, the aggregate purchasing power in the deficit country is in no way affected by balance-of-payments deficits, however large they may be.

Undoubtedly, domestic purchasing power is affected by other influences, especially those that operate through credit policy. It is at all times the result of a great number of factors, more or less independent of each other. In particular, domestic inflation can check and even reverse the contraction of purchasing power which, under the gold standard, results from any balance-of-payments deficit.

But, subject to this reservation, one must note that even in cases where the national income is strictly equal in value to the national product (that is to say, when there is no inflation), the gold-exchange standard totally dissociates aggregate purchasing power from the balance-of-payments outcome. It thereby removes the regulating influence that the monetary mechanism would have under the gold standard.

Thus, under the gold-exchange standard, a country's balance of payments is no longer affected by the settlements to which it gives rise. It can only be expected to find its equilibrium, even in the most favorable circumstances, through a systematic credit policy or the imposition of import controls.

But experience has shown time and again that it is, if not impossible, at least very difficult for monetary authorities to achieve systematically by way of authoritative decisions the credit shrinkage that in effect the gold standard made unnecessary.

As to the manipulation of the balance of payments by such means as restriction on foreign spending or restricted currency allowances to tourists, or even prohibition on movements of capital, to my knowledge, this has always been a failure.

The layman is sometimes surprised to see the decisive effect that aggregate variations in purchasing power have on the balance-of-payments outcome. This is not the place to analyze this phenomenon in detail. Suffice it to say that any excess at a given time of aggregate domestic demand over aggregate domestic production tends to hold aggregate domestic production back at home. And any difference in the opposite direction tends to free for export part of the wealth offered for sale in the market.

Over the past ten years, whenever the balance-of-payments situation has been restored in France or in Britain, this has always been brought about by a contraction in the income level. It has never been accomplished by bringing any direct government action to bear upon the various components of foreign trade.

A second consequence is that under the gold-exchange standard, any deficit in the balance of payments of a country whose currency

is returned to it—the United States and, in the sterling area, Britain
—produces a duplication of the world's credit base.

Indeed, the foreign exchange transferred for the settlement of the
deficit is bought, against the creation of money, by the banking
system of the creditor country. The cash holdings thus generated
are handed over to the creditors of the debtor country.

But at the same time, these amounts in foreign currency against
which the creditor country has created money are reinvested in the
market of the debtor country. Thus everything happens as if these
amounts had never left the debtor country.

Thus these foreign-exchange amounts representing the balance-
of-payments deficit flow into the credit system of the creditor
country, while at the same time remaining in the debtor country,
thereby giving rise to a straightforward duplication phenomenon.

Through this mechanism, the substitution of the gold-exchange
standard for the gold standard—which in a period when payments
were roughly in balance would not have much effect on aggregate
purchasing power—becomes a powerful instrument of worldwide
inflation the moment large migrations of international capital occur.

The above analysis has been proved absolutely but tragically
true by the events that preceded and followed the 1929 recession.

As already stated, the financial rehabilitation that was effected
in Germany and France had brought a massive influx of capital
from overseas to these two countries between 1925 and 1929.

But both of these countries were in fact operating under the
gold-exchange standard, which gave an exceptional impetus to the
1929 boom as a result of the credit-duplication phenomenon that
is one of its main characteristics.

The movements of capital from the United States to Germany
and France during the years 1958–1960 have caused, through the
same mechanism, an exceptional liquidity increase. This has been
and is still reflected in an abnormal rise in the prices of stocks and
shares in financial markets.

When capital flows back from countries where it took refuge
to countries whence it originated, you can have a boom in the latter

without having a recession in the former. Those in the first group have an inducement effect on those of the second, where there is nothing to restrain the boom. Thus all the countries that have adopted the gold-exchange standard find themselves carried away on a powerful wave of inflationary expansion, which affects the economy or the stock exchange.

The above findings are in no way incompatible with theories that see in salary increases not matched by a rise in productivity the origin of the process of inflation, and consider that cost-push inflation is quite different from demand-pull inflation. Although it is often difficult in such a case to separate cause from effect, there is no doubt that the constant increase in total purchasing power causes and justifies wage claims while removing all obstacles to their successful outcome.

The third and most serious consequence of the gold-exchange standard is the fallacious nature of the credit structure to which it gives rise.

In the message mentioned above, President Kennedy noted that at the end of 1960 the $17.5 billion gold reserve of the United States served as backing for $20 million of foreign short-term or sight assets on the one hand and, on the other, for the $11.5 billion representing the U.S. domestic money supply.

I do not claim that the existing gold stock is not sufficient in present circumstances to guarantee the currency of the United States. In fact, President Kennedy has stated his intention to reduce, through a modification of existing regulations, the amount of gold required as backing for the money in circulation.

In addition, the dollar could draw for support on several assets not yet used—especially the U.S. drawing rights on the International Monetary Fund, as well as large assets abroad.

It is not the value of the dollar that the above findings put to doubt. They only force one to note that the operation of the gold-exchange standard, during periods of large capital migrations, will establish a double mortgage, amounting to a very big sum, on an important part of the gold stock of the United States. If foreigners requested payment in gold for a substantial part of their dollar holdings, they could really bring about a collapse of the credit structure in the United States.

Assuredly, they will not do so. But the simple fact that they have the right to do it forces us to recall that it was the collapse of the house of cards built on the gold-exchange standard in Europe that turned the recession of 1929 into a Great Depression.

In 1960 the same circumstances are present, although on a different scale. If we are not careful, the same causes could produce the same effects. Therefore, it is absolutely necessary, before it is too late, to correct the situation resulting from the dual pyramidal credit structure based on the world gold stock.

### 3. How To Get Away from This System

Getting out of a system based on the gold-exchange standard, after a prolonged period of its operation between a large number of countries, raises two problems:

—Substituting for the monetary system existing in these countries a system that will not favor or sustain the deficit of countries whose currencies are considered as equal to gold by the banks of issue which receive them.

—Eliminating a situation rendered dangerously vulnerable by the duplication of the credit structure erected on the gold stock of countries with a currency regarded as equivalent to gold.

As regards the future, any system to be established should prevent creditor countries from receiving, in settlement of their claims, a purchasing power that the debtor countries have not lost. To this end, no bank of issue should be allowed to lend a foreign creditor the foreign exchange against which it has already created purchasing power in its own currency.

Some major countries, like the United States and Britain, follow a practice that fulfills this condition and therefore fully meets the above requirement. Their banks of issue refuse to include in their assets substantial foreign-exchange reserves and, as a result, issue currency only against gold or against claims denominated in the national currency.

However, other multilateral clearing systems could meet the requirement if the balances arising out of the settlement of the deficits were not again placed at the disposal of the deficit country, as for example through a short-term loan in its money market.

However, such sterilization would always be precarious, because of its deliberate and costly nature, whereas sterilization resulting from the operation of the gold standard is the unconditional and unavoidable consequence of the rules that characterize it.

The evolution of the European Payments Union, through the progressive hardening of its method of settlement—that is, by the increase of the gold part of the settlements which it effected— provides an example of a gradual move toward a system based on the gold standard.

To eliminate the dangers that threaten the Western world as a result of fifteen years of the gold-exchange standard, there is unfortunately no other solution for the West than to repay in gold the greater part of the claims in dollars that have accumulated in the assets of the banks of issue. Only such reimbursement can remove the risks of a collapse or of sudden deflation, inherent in the duplication of the credit structure erected on the gold reserve of the United States.

The difficulty of the operation lies in the sudden reduction that such repayment would impose on the gold reserves of the Federal Reserve System.

However, the situation is less serious than it appears to be. President Kennedy himself has listed the resources available or likely to be made available for such reimbursement if requested.

In addition, the liquidation of the gold-exchange standard, if it does not result from panic—which is precisely what must be avoided—can only be organized and effected progressively.

However, the elimination of the duplication typical of the gold-exchange standard, by eliminating dollars from cash holdings of the banks of issue, will reduce the aggregate volume of monetary

liquidity. And it may well reduce it to a level less than the minimum amount needed for day-to-day settlements.

Such a consequence would not be accepted. To prevent it,
several proposals have been put forward, the best known being
that of Professor Triffin.

This ingenious plan, similar to the one presented by Lord
Keynes in 1943,[3] would considerably reduce the liquidity requirements of the central banks as a result of the concentration of cash
holdings. But, under the complex system envisaged by Professor
Triffin, the new currency prescribed for settlements would be only
partially convertible and, in certain circumstances, might have to
be enforced. In addition, the issuing authority, because of its right
of issue, would have a right to effect levies on the economies of
member states.

It was fear of inflation that caused the rejection of the Keynes
plan in 1943. The same objections still seem valid today against
several other plans that are more or less the same kettle of fish.

The rejection of an inflationary solution has led certain commentators to seek the augmentation of the nominal value of gold
holdings through an increase in the price of gold. They observe that
this price has remained unchanged at its 1934 level of $35 per
ounce in spite of the fact that prices in dollars have just about
doubled since then.

There is no doubt that an increase in the price of gold expressed
in dollars—and therefore in the price of gold in all currencies whose
rate has been fixed in dollars—would increase the nominal value
of the gold reserves. This would facilitate the liquidation of spurious cash holdings that have arisen out of the operation of the gold-
exchange standard.

However, it would be rash to use over-simple calculations in
estimating how much of a rise there should be, or even merely to
contend that an increase could not be avoided.

First, the extension and improvement of existing clearing institutions would materially reduce cash requirements.

---

[3] *Proposals by Experts for an International Clearing Union.*

On the other hand, it is false to say that the production of gold is not substantially affected both by the price assigned to it and by the movements of the general price level.

The above remarks indicate that the necessary liquidation of the gold-exchange standard raises difficult problems—of political craft on the one hand and of monetary technique on the other. These call for thorough study and discussion.

In preparation for such discussion, it is essential to realize that the problems are neither exclusively, nor even essentially, American. Their solution can only be found in a thorough modification of the existing system for the settlement of the balance of international exchanges, and therefore of the practices now followed by the national banks of issue.

While the gold-exchange standard is mainly responsible for the U.S. balance-of-payments deficit, it was not the United States but the International Monetary Conference of 1922 that was responsible for its widespread extension.

What has been done by an international conference can only be undone by an international conference. But it must be undone quickly. A monetary crisis would jeopardize the financial rehabilitation that has finally been achieved in all Western countries. It would expose their economies to a serious recession, which in turn would carry with it all the dangers of a Great Depression.

In any case, the problem of the gold-exchange standard is sure to be settled in the not too distant future, be it during a critical or a quiet period. It is essential that it be settled during a quiet period. To this end, government initiative is urgently needed. If it comes in time it will spare the peoples of the West the tribulations and sufferings of a new world crisis.


ADDITIONAL CONSIDERATIONS CONCERNING
THE GOLD-EXCHANGE STANDARD

The existence of a certain amount of money, whether in the form of bank notes or of credit balances with the bank, is always the outcome of the purchase by a bank—the bank of issue or any commercial bank—of an asset of equal value. In the balance sheet, that monetized asset is shown on the assets side and the amount of money that expresses it is shown as an item of liability.

The requirement that the two corresponding items should always be of equal value is basic, because the equilibrium of the balance sheet of the bank of issue, and in particular the possibility for that bank to mop up the amount of liquidity created when it is no longer desired, hinges on this requirement being met.

The result of this requirement is that the list of assets that can be monetized is limited to those with a fixed value in terms of the national currency. Where the national currency is fully convertible into gold, these items are gold itself at legal par value and, under any system whatsoever, claims denominated in the national currency which always regain their face value when they come to maturity. Thus, under the gold standard, the statutes of the bank of issue limit the assets that it is empowered to buy to gold and to short-term claims denominated in the national currency. The time limit provides an assurance that, day after day, bills whose aggregate value is no less than the cash holdings to be reabsorbed will come to maturity, or in other words will regain the value level at which they had been purchased.

The idea developed that foreign currencies which were freely convertible into gold—but only to the extent that they remained so convertible—met the requirement relating to immutable value in terms of the national currency, and could for that reason be accepted as a component of the reserve base. From this idea the gold-exchange standard was evolved as an adjunct to, rather than a substitute for, the gold standard.

Resolution 9 of the International Monetary Conference held in Genoa in 1922 recommended the conclusion of an international convention "for savings in the use of gold by maintaining reserves in the form of foreign balances."

Clearly the inclusion of foreign balances in the monetized assets of the banks of issue constituted a saving in the use of gold, because it reduced by a corresponding amount the quantity of gold held against a certain quantity of money.

The fear of a gold shortage haunted the minds of Anglo-Saxon economists after the First World War. Toward 1927 or 1928 the Financial Committee of the League of Nations was to establish a "gold delegation" with the task of devising ways and means of remedying a gold shortage. This anxiety was in fact fully justified. Prices in terms of gold (i.e., prices in the United States) had increased by about 50 percent since 1914 as a result of the gold inflow into the country that had been the prime supplier of the belligerents. So long as the United States could hold on to its increased gold reserves, it would be in a position to maintain monetary convertibility, which in fact did not exist in any other country. But equally clearly, the moment other states endeavored to replenish their gold reserves—and Britain had restored convertibility on the basis of the prewar par value as early as 1925—the quantity of gold available would be inadequate.

At that time the world-famous economist Charles Rist had already shown that, with regard to the 50 percent increase in prices in terms of gold, widespread restoration of the convertibility of national currencies required that the gold price be restored to its rightful place in the price hierarchy. That is, it should be pegged up by about 50 percent.

However, as is the case today, public opinion in Anglo-Saxon countries, in particular in the United States, was obstinately opposed to a rise in the price of gold. The Genoa experts recommended economizing in the use of gold by resorting to the system that was to become the gold-exchange standard. This was only an artificial device to eke out by dollar and sterling balances the unduly low nominal value of the existing gold stocks—the unavoidable outcome of holding the gold price at an artificial level.

The same situation recurred, *mutatis mutandis*, in 1945. It was as a result of a similar situation and for the same reasons that the gold-exchange standard, which had vanished in the throes of the Great Depression, rose from its ashes.

To the extent that private banks create money in the form of credit balances in their books, one can rightly claim that when they own in their assets foreign currencies convertible into gold, there are always traces of the gold-exchange standard, even in the strictest of the gold-standard systems.

Under such systems, the banks of issue are the only ones that are prohibited, by virtue of their statutes, from holding assets or claims in foreign currencies.

The Bank of France was in such a situation prior to 7 April 1926, on which date it was given "authority to purchase gold, silver, and foreign currencies in the market." Such authority was rescinded by the Monetary Act of 29 June 1928, in pursuance of which the Treasury was substituted for the Bank as regards the purchase of foreign exchange offered for sale in the market.

The Legislative Decree of 30 June 1937, amending the Monetary Act of 1 October 1936, provided that the Exchange Stabilization Fund "would be entrusted with the task of regularizing the relationship between the French franc and foreign currencies . . . the Bank of France being empowered to sell gold and foreign currencies to the Exchange Stabilization Fund or purchase them from that Fund." It was therefore in 1936 that the gold-exchange standard became legal again in France.

Between 25 June 1928 and 30 June 1937, the system applied in France was the gold standard. But if one is to interpret the operation of this system correctly, one must observe that the exclusion of the gold-exchange standard obviously does not prevent the bank of issue from receiving foreign exchange in its daily transactions. Such a system merely compels the bank to surrender foreign exchange to the state or to request the debtor bank of issue to convert it into gold. But it must be observed that this latter obligation is mitigated by the need for any bank to maintain in its vault the amount of foreign exchange necessary to meet its requirements for day-to-day or foreseeable settlements.

Specific situations induced Britain to follow systematically a gold-exchange standard policy with respect to some of its creditors.

Before 1914, for instance, it relied systematically on the retention of sterling balances by several dominions or various Latin American countries.[4]

For the above reasons, no monetary system is absolutely free from any trace of the gold-exchange standard. But what characterizes systems based on the gold standard and distinguishes them from systems based on the gold-exchange standard is that the ratio of foreign exchange to total bank reserves, and in particular central-bank reserves, remains very limited.

Thus, on balance, I would say that it is this particular ratio that characterizes the monetary system. When the ratio is very low, the system is in fact a gold-standard system; when it is high or very high, we have a gold-exchange system.

To illustrate my point, I would make it clear that in 1965 the system followed in France was indisputably a gold-exchange system. The balance sheet of the Bank of France as of 7 January 1965 showed foreign cash balances in the amount of 20,666,-300,000 francs, as against gold reserves in the amount of 4,300,-226,000 francs. The proportion of foreign exchange in the total assets of the balance sheet was about 34 percent.

[4] See the lecture by Mr. Lebée in *Les Doctrines monétaires à l'épreuve des faits* (Paris: Alcan, 1932), p. 134.

# II

___

## CAN THE MONETARY SYSTEM OF THE WEST ENDURE?

The three articles that I published in June 1961 aroused violent reactions.

For the information of some people in high office who had shown an interest in them, and for several friends, I drew up a more detailed, more technical note in January 1962. Unpublished until now, it is reproduced here.

My articles on the gold-exchange standard aroused comments and criticism that considerably enriched my analysis. As I cannot possibly thank the authors individually, let me present here some of the most outstanding of these observations and criticisms, and expound the lessons I have derived from them and the reflections they have prompted.

To repeat my contention: the gold-exchange standard enables banks of issue to enter in their assets, as a counterpart of the money they issue, not only gold and claims denominated in the national currency—as is the case with the gold standard—but also foreign exchange payable in gold. The effect has been not merely—as people too often believe—to impart more flexibility to the system of metal convertibility common to all Western countries, but to alter its consequences considerably.

The fact that the recipient banks of issue retain claims expressed in particular foreign currencies, which are called key currencies (and which are in fact the dollar and, within the sterling area, the pound sterling itself), has three basic consequences:

—It eliminates in the key-currency countries the constriction of domestic purchasing power, which under the gold standard resulted, *ceteris paribus*, from any balance-of-payments deficit and which tended to correct such a deficit.

—It causes any capital transfer from key-currency countries to other countries to generate an increase in purchasing power, which is in no way associated with an increase in the value of goods that can be purchased, nor with the requirements of economic expansion.

—It exposes convertible-currency countries as a whole to the risk of a recession, which would result from a collapse of the dual-pyramidal credit structure generated by the gold-exchange standard.


## THE GOLD-EXCHANGE STANDARD AND
## MONETARY POLICY

That there is a problem with the gold-exchange standard has been abundantly borne out by balance-of-payments difficulties that have brought or bring pressure to bear on the dollar or the pound. None of my commentators has denied this. But they differ from me—with considerable variations in their individual views—in their assessment of the seriousness and urgency of the problem and their evaluation of the methods for resolving it.

1. Some reprove me for bringing out the deficiencies of the monetary system of the West at a time when the international situation calls for a major production endeavor that only confidence in the future can bring about.

I met with similar objections in the latter part of 1958. They were raised by those who criticized me for having expressed the wish that French finances be rehabilitated, notwithstanding the financial burdens that the war in Algeria was imposing on the nation.

I am of the opposite view. When an exceptional effort is needed, it is an overriding obligation that the country be put in a position where such an effort can be sustained as long as is necessary. I am convinced that when a storm threatens, it is particularly urgent to check the rigging.

Let me hear no more that by trying to ward off the dangers of a storm, you may well provoke it. Even though you may deny its eventuality, it will surely break one day, and he that wants to ride it through must brace himself as promptly as possible to resist it.

2. Several critics recognize the dangers inherent in the duplication of purchasing power that transfers of capital from key-currency countries involve, *ceteris paribus*, under the gold-exchange system. However, they observe that such a system has no consequences of any kind—and therefore no perverse effect—where there are no such transfers, i.e., where the balance of payments of key-currency countries is in equilibrium.

There is no need, they say, to consider eliminating the gold-exchange standard, since this system will have no adverse effect the moment key-currency countries agree to bring their balance of payments into equilibrium.

Dissenters who so argue fall into two groups as regards their opinion on the way a balance-of-payments equilibrium can be attained in key-currency countries.

The first category consists of those who believe more or less consciously that a country can shape its balance of payments by authoritative or incentive measures and thereby bring it into equilibrium.

Assuredly, government powers vary depending upon the nature of their international operations. They carry greater freedom of action when one finds on the debit side—as is the case with the U.S.

balance of payments—major donations or loans whose maintenance hinges only on a political decision. But even in such cases, experience reveals that there is in the balance of international commitments a hard core that it is extremely difficult to reduce. A reduction on the debit side nearly always entails a corresponding reduction on the credit side, so that the balance remains unchanged. Such a correlation is hardly surprising. It is easily explained by balance-of-payments theory.

In any case, the experience of France and Britain has shown on repeated occasions over the past ten years the inefficacy of methods designed to reduce the balance-of-payments deficit by direct intervention in the field of international operations. Prior to 1958, France tried every possible device: general quota restrictions on imports, reduction and even elimination of foreign-exchange allocations to tourists, export subsidies, export incentives made effective by the most refined methods. But they all failed: the balance of payments remained serenely in deficit. On the other hand, the reforms of 27 December 1958, which put an end to inflation, were enough to generate a balance-of-payments surplus.

It may well be that a fully planned system can shape balances of payments at will. It should be made clear, however, that notwithstanding all the powers vested in him, Dr. Schacht did not succeed in bringing this about. And it was Stalin himself who advocated the "control of the economy through the ruble."

That is why several of my detractors—that is, those in the second group—who expected the restoration of equilibrium in the U.S. balance of payments to eliminate the drawbacks inherent in the gold-exchange standard, are fully aware that equilibrium in international transactions cannot be expected to result from a manipulation of their various components. Fully aware of the repeated lessons derived from French and British experience, they appreciate that such equilibrium can only be brought about by action affecting aggregate purchasing power, with a view to eliminating any excess of aggregate demand over the aggregate value of total supplies, that is, the elimination of the inflationary gap.

This method, for its part, has always proved effective, and Mr. Selwyn Lloyd has recently applied it once more—and very vigorously—in the case of Britain.

Yet the proponents of this approach observe that while aggregate purchasing power is affected by the settlement of the international trade balance under the gold standard, it is also influenced—and more directly—by the credit policy. They also say, quite rightly, that the overall impact of all such influences, and that impact alone, affects aggregate purchasing power and, through the level at which the latter is established, the balance of payments itself.

The relevance of this concept cannot be doubted. I had myself made it clear in the French text of my articles that "domestic purchasing power was affected by influences other than those resulting from the balance-of-payments settlement, in particular by credit policy, and that *inter alia* domestic inflation could offset and even reverse the reduction in purchasing power which, under the gold standard, resulted from any balance-of-payments deficit." While this qualification on my part was watered down in the translation that appeared in *Fortune* magazine, nevertheless its relevance remains unimpaired.

There is no doubt that by means of credit restrictions or open market interventions—for instance, by selling Treasury bills in the market—the bank of issue of a key-currency country can bring about, under the gold-exchange standard, a reduction in aggregate purchasing power identical to that which, under the gold standard, would have resulted from the settlement of the international trade balance.

I do not propose to describe the phenomenon which such an impulse would trigger off. It would be much more complex than is generally recognized in the over-simple contentions based on the quantitative theory of money. I have, however, outlined them in two previous studies.[1]

---

[1] "Influences Regulating the Amount of Currency and the Institutional Problem of Money," *Revue d'économie politique*, 1953 and one pamphlet in the *Recueil Sirey*, 1953; but primarily "Théorie du taux d'escompte et de la

But whatever it comprises, the overall phenomenon will be unleashed with all attendant consequences by any reduction in aggregate demand, whether such a reduction is the mechanical result of the settlement of a balance-of-payments deficit under the gold standard, other things being equal, or the result under any other system of a purposeful decision by credit policymakers. Although it must be stressed that, in this latter case, balance-of-payments equilibrium can only be restored to the extent that the reduction is by the same amount as it would have been in the former case.

At this point, however, I must observe that, contrary to the views held by several of my critics—and even by the most eminent among them—the option seems to me purely theoretical.

I do not believe, as a matter of fact, that the monetary authorities, however courageous and well informed they may be, can deliberately bring about those contractions in the money supply that the mere mechanism of the gold standard would have generated automatically.

Such contractions, if they are to be effective, must reduce domestic demand by an amount equal to the balance-of-payments deficit. Their purpose and effect is therefore to prevent the home population from consuming a part of domestic production that must be made available for export.

It is precisely because it eliminates the consequence which, under the gold standard, tends to result from a balance-of-payments deficit that the gold-exchange standard is considered useful.

Can one conceive that the monetary or fiscal authorities should in all circumstances be able to achieve deliberately and consciously what it was intended they should not have to do as a result of the substitution of the gold-exchange standard for the gold standard? Moreover, what would have been the beneficial effect of such a substitution if in any case it was to be devoid of any consequence whatsoever?

---

balance des comptes," *Revue économique* (Armand Colin, 1957). Both are reproduced in *Balance of Payments* (New York: Macmillan, 1967), pp. 133–264.

Even assuming that, under the gold-exchange standard, the monetary and fiscal authorities set out—with rare courage—to achieve through the credit policy what settlement of the balance-of-payments deficit would have achieved automatically under the gold standard, they could not possibly succeed, at least at the right time.

This is in fact demonstrated by a highly significant document, the report of a group of experts who had been asked by the Secretary-General of the OEEC to report on the "problem of rising prices," in pursuance of a resolution of the Council dated 12 June 1959.

The report, dated 31 May 1961, observes as follows as regards the regulation of demand by the monetary and fiscal authorities:

> There is nothing inherently inadequate about the available monetary and fiscal policy instruments, but their weakness comes from lack of decision to use them firmly and promptly. . . . It was a case of too little and too late. . . . We were struck by the fact that for many countries there remain major gaps and serious delays in the information that the authorities should have as a guide to prompt and adequate policy decisions.

In point of fact, I very much doubt the feasibility of securing promptly the detailed and reliable information required for the implementation of a reasoned credit policy. I had occasion to participate, with two of my colleagues, in the administration of the exchange stabilization fund for many months in 1937–1938. My experience was that when faced with any shift in the rates of exchange, it was difficult, if not impossible, to determine whether such a shift was a reflection of long-term variations or of mere market fluctuations.

Contractions in the credit supply often hurt the people whom they affect. Is it not, therefore, to be expected that those in whose power it is to produce them should not bring them about until and unless they are fully assured that such contractions are absolutely necessary? What happens is that they often abstain, and when eventually they decide to act, their action is nearly always too late or too limited.

I call upon my colleagues and friends who are "the monetary or fiscal authorities" and who, I know, are fully devoted to the public interest and are quite courageous, to say in all conscience whether they feel in a position to set in motion credit restrictions sufficient to offset a balance-of-payments deficit—that is, equivalent to those that would have been set in motion by the effective settlement of the debit balances—with the speed and on the scale that would have characterized the internal consequences of the deficit under the gold standard.

3. However, while maintaining the balance-of-payments deficit in key-currency countries, the gold-exchange standard does not prevent the deficit from making its effects fully felt. It automatically and inexorably siphons off the gold and foreign-exchange reserves of such countries, so that after a certain period of time their governments are faced with the option of having either to institute general import quota restrictions and severe controls on foreign-exchange movements, or to restore balance-of-payments equilibrium.

Until now, the Western countries, having relied on the first of these methods and having promptly experienced its inefficacy, have had no choice but to fall back on the second. But as they could not be content with mere words, they have had no alternative but to reduce domestic purchasing power, as the gold standard would have done.

By taking the courageous course advocated by Selwyn Lloyd on 26 July 1961, Britain imposed upon itself very severe restrictions on purchasing power. Although the situation was promptly reversed as a result of the measures taken, it is too early yet to pass judgment on the nature of the recovery that they induced. It must be noted, however, that on several occasions since the end of the war, Britain in such situations has resorted to the same procedure, which has always proved effective.

Thus, nations that desire their balance of payments to be in

equilibrium eventually find that there is no way out but to deliberately and consciously effect the contractions in the purchasing
power that the free play of the gold standard would have brought
about. However, while the two approaches may yield equivalent
results, they involve very different modalities of action and have
very different social and human repercussions.

The first approach—i.e., the one involved in the operation of
the gold standard—is followed daily and its application is therefore
limited, as regards the size of the changes in the purchasing power
which it brings on, to the amount of the net balance of external
settlements effected daily. The changes it generates are therefore
slow and gradual. Their effects are hardly perceptible from the
social point of view.

On the other hand, the second approach aims at offsetting in one
single operation the cumulative effect of excess purchasing power,
often of protracted duration. The reduction in the purchasing power must be all the more substantial as it has long been postponed.
But in every circumstance, if it is to be effective, it must bring on
a deflation of considerable magnitude. It subjects the economy to
a sort of shock treatment and has a painful social impact.

In addition, it can only be followed in a given political context
which does not always exist and which, in any case, is always influenced by the backlash effects resulting from the rehabilitation
operation proper.

Can one really evade the obligation of asking oneself—and asking the monetary and political authorities—whether it is wise to
turn down regulating influences that are hardly perceptible but
always effective (unless, of course, they are offset by concomitant
variations)? Will it not only be necessary at a later stage to impose,
during monetary and political upheavals, disruptions more painful and of wider scope than those which the tutelary mechanism
of the gold standard would have brought on unobtrusively and
only to the extent necessary?

4. Several commentators recognize that the gold-exchange standard turns any transfer of capital from a key-currency country

to other countries into a factor that increases aggregate purchasing power in the convertible-currency countries taken as a whole. Yet they consider this feature not a drawback but a major benefit.[2]

Failing such consequences, they say, the rapid increase in production could not have been financed, in the absence of the discovery of new gold deposits. Several other commentators go one step further and contend that the gold-exchange standard itself is the one factor that generates expansion, through the credit facilities that it creates.

The two lines of argument must be considered separately.

As regards the first, it should be observed that, due to the substantial credit margin that they involve, monetary systems based on gold are endowed with considerable flexibility and afford broad opportunities for contracyclical action by the monetary authorities. The magnitude of the gold base, for its part, is much influenced by variations in the general price levels, as gold production increases when the general price level decreases and declines when the general price level rises.

Such regulating influences can be seen to exist and their effectiveness can be gauged if one simply observes that the general price level in terms of gold in 1910 was substantially the same as in 1890, notwithstanding the tremendous economic expansion that had occurred in the intervening period, requiring a threefold increase in the monetary gold stock to maintain the general price level. The chart appended to the report of the Gold Delegation of the Financial Committee of the League of Nations (Geneva, 1932) shows that this variation cannot be regarded as purely fortuitous and that it was the direct result of variations in the price index in terms of gold.

It goes without saying, however, that the effectiveness of such regulating influences would be considerably affected by a notable shift in the cost of gold production as compared with the price at

---

[2] "In fact," says one of the most prominent of these commentators, "the severing of the automatic link between reserve movements and changes in the money supply is a principal advantage of the present standard."

which gold is purchased by the banks of issue. Since the price of gold expressed in dollars was last pegged up in 1934, the general price level expressed in dollars has practically doubled. Can one imagine what would have happened to wheat production if, in terms of dollars, wheat prices had been maintained at their 1933 level? However, the introduction of more efficient mining techniques has partly offset this disparity, to an extent which only an exhaustive survey could determine. This therefore poses a major problem, whose eventuality the Articles of Agreement of the Internation Monetary Fund forsaw and which they could easily solve.

The second line of argument is championed by those who hold the view that there can be no growth without inflation. This is not the place for discussing the validity of this argument. Let me simply observe that acceptance of this view is no justification for relying on fully unpredictable and generally fortuitous capital shifts to bring about economic growth in convertible-currency countries. The great expansion of credit that brought about the 1927–1929 boom was due to the fact that Germany and France had restored their financial situation in the years 1924–1928 as a result of a combination of purely political circumstances. Similarly, the major credit expansion and the rise in prices of stocks and shares that characterized the years 1959–1961 were due to the fact that Germany and France had restored financial stability after the Korean War, in the case of Germany, and in December 1958, as regards France.

The inflation brought on by the gold-exchange standard is all the more undesirable as it is necessarily limited in scope and duration. As it accumulates short-term claims against the gold reserves of key-currency countries, and as such claims compete with the concurrent claims of domestic circulation to those same reserves, it inevitably leads, if it lasts for any length of time, to two possible outcomes: a collapse or a forced currency.

To summarize, the gold-exchange standard places the whole economy in the situation of a man falling from the tenth floor: everything goes well at the start, but he can be sure that he is going to crash to the ground.

In view of the above considerations, the gold-exchange standard cannot be accepted as an instrument for economic expansion. Anyone wanting to secure expansion through inflation must not rely on an uncontrollable and indiscriminate procedure. He must have the courage to take personal responsibility for its implementation and administration by means of an appropriate credit policy.

The gold-exchange standard is a misleading disguise that gives inflation the honest appearance of a procedure for the settlement of international liabilities. If central banks want inflation because they expect it to result in expansion, let them have it overtly and in broad daylight. They should not rely on capital shifts to bring it about for them on the sly.

5. Several commentators are of the opinion that the 1961 situation is quite different from the situation that existed in 1929. Indeed, since 1934 the United States has no longer been committed to supplying gold to all dollar-holders, but only to foreign monetary authorities (governments and central banks) "for legitimate monetary purposes."

This restriction would have the effect of excepting U.S. gold from claims on it resulting from the existence of private foreign holdings. It would also enable the monetary authorities to appreciate the merits of requests for repayment in gold that might be submitted to them. Furthermore, even this last precaution would not be absolutely necessary because central banks, by virtue of their high tradition of international solidarity, could not possibly be expected to behave irresponsibly or to jeopardize the solvency of their debtors by untimely requests for repayment.

Who could fail to realize the fragility of such safeguards? Private dollar-holders can always secure reimbursement by surrendering to their central bank. Any attempt to discriminate between requests depending upon the purposes for which they are submitted would in fact create a black market in the dollar.

Lastly, while central banks have an international responsibility to fulfill, they are also responsible toward holders of the currency that they themselves have issued. It would be neither wise nor safe to place them in too serious a dilemma between these two types of responsibilities.

I am not prepared to concede that by conjuring up such hazards I am putting dollar stability in jeopardy. All those who have given some thought to the problem are aware of such dangers. My aim is to banish fallacious safeguards so as to rely only on effective guarantees.

6. Some critics were surprised that I came to the conclusion that an international conference should be convened to make arrangements for the elimination of the gold-exchange standard. The answer is simple: the inflation engendered by the gold-exchange standard does not affect a specific country, but all convertible-currency countries in the aggregate. If convertibility is to recapture all its virtues, then all banks of issue that practice it must undertake simultaneously to cease accumulating foreign exchange in their assets. Such a commitment, however, calls for an international agreement. The procedures to be followed to arrive at such an agreement are immaterial.

## THE GOLD-EXCHANGE STANDARD AND
## THE COURSE OF HISTORY

Many of my critics complain that my analysis, by setting up the shortcomings of the gold-exchange standard as against the virtues of the gold standard, is backward and outmoded.

The *Cahiers de la République,* for example, reproaches me with attempting to revive a corpse.[3]

Raymond Aron is of the opinion that "the gold standard is a thing of the past, like sailing ships and oil lamps."[4]

*The Economist* considers that "there is no ordered way of putting the clock back. Gold: gold exchange standard: key cur-

[3] August 1961.
[4] *Le Figaro,* 5 July 1961.

rencies backed by IMF: true international credit—this is a natural progression [for the monetary system of the West]."[5]

All the above contentions are based on the notion that the gold-exchange standard was substituted for the gold standard because it represented a relative advance. But the facts categorically invalidate such a claim. Resolution 9 of the Genoa Conference, which in 1922 recommended that it be introduced, states expressly that the gold-exchange standard "makes for savings in the use of gold by maintaining reserves in the form of foreign balances."

The Genoa experts held the view that the gold-exchange standard was only an expedient, a gimmick, which did not operate so as to improve the functioning of the world monetary system in a lasting manner. Instead, it was expected to stave off the gold shortage that would have resulted, in the then existing conditions, from the restoration of gold convertibility in those countries which had abandoned such convertibility during the First World War.

For all those who examined the situation that had arisen out of the war, a shortage of gold reserves was obviously something to be feared. For *de jure* or *de facto* reasons, banks of issue maintain a certain ratio between the currency value of their gold holdings and the quantity of money that they have issued in the form of banknotes or of credit balances in their books. It is this ratio that constituted what was then called the percentage cover.

As to the quantities of money, they too are roughly commensurate with the level of prices.

Between 1913 and 1920, the average level of wholesale prices in terms of gold rose from 110 to 244[6] and total demand liabilities of central banks rose from $1,226 million to $4,299 million.

With the then existing level of reserves, such increases should have made it impossible to maintain gold convertibility, thereby affording a practical demonstration of the inadequacy of the gold reserves. In fact, however, the dollar had remained convertible

[5] 8 July 1961, p. 152.
[6] Provisional report by the Gold Delegation of the Financial Committee of the League of Nations, 1930.

into gold throughout the war and could still be freely converted in 1920. Yet this situation, which was apparently abnormal, was due to a peculiar combination of circumstances.

In the first place, inflation had caused the disappearance of gold coins—a well-known phenomenon. The suspension of gold convertibility in all the belligerent countries, with the exception of the United States, brought about a situation where the United States alone was paying the agreed price for gold. At the same time, due to the events of the war, the United States had become the main source of supplies for the Allies. These and several other factors caused gold to flow into the vaults of the Federal Reserve System, whose metal reserves increased from $4,922 million in 1913 to $7,652 million in 1920.[7]

This concentration of gold in the United States made it possible, notwithstanding the changed situation as a result of the war, to maintain throughout the world the gold convertibility of one currency, i.e., the dollar. But everything pointed to the conclusion that the price to be paid for maintaining such convertibility was the inconvertibility of all other major currencies. And that any endeavor hindering the concentration of gold in the vaults of the Federal Reserve System—and in particular the restoration of sterling and French franc convertibility—would reveal the inadequacy of world gold stocks in relation to existing price levels, and therefore the impossibility of reverting to the prewar monetary system.

Now, in 1920, all the major countries that had instituted forced currency during the war were determined to restore gold convertibility at the prewar par value at the earliest possible date. Britain, in fact, restored it in 1925. And France itself, notwithstanding the substantial depreciation of its currency, had undertaken the self-imposed obligation–incorporated in legislation specifically to that effect—to restore it within a very short period, contrary to the dictates of common sense.

Thus, in 1920 there was no doubt that the value of the gold

[7] *Op. cit.*

stocks available would not make it possible to implement the desired and stated policy of the major countries. The policy could only be feasible if there was a substantial increase in the currency value of the available gold stock or a modification of practices relating to monetary convertibility, bringing on a notable saving in the amount of gold reserves required for the carrying out of such policy.

The first of the above two solutions could manifestly have been brought about by a reduction in the legal gold content of the dollar, in other words, by an increase in the price of gold in terms of dollars. Such an increase would have augmented by a corresponding amount the currency value of the gold holdings. It also could have brought them up to the level required for a general return of currencies to convertibility, subject to the adoption of an appropriate rate of exchange in countries where price levels were not equivalent to those obtaining in the United States.

In 1920, however, no change was envisaged in the definition of the gold content of the major currencies, that is, in the legal determination of the quantity of gold that they represented. What is more, such a change was formally ruled out not only in the United States, where the price levels obtaining in 1920 were twice the prewar levels, but also in Britain, where they had increased threefold—and in France, where they had risen fivefold.

Thus the solution of an increase in the nominal value of existing gold stocks through an increase in the price of gold was ruled out. And there was no alternative—if the intention was to pursue a policy of return to gold convertibility—but to change the convertibility practices followed, thereby bringing about a notable saving in the quantities of gold that convertibility required. The gold-exchange standard afforded such a saving, making it possible to extract two cumulative monetary accounting operations from a single gold stock by entering in the reserve both the gold content of such stock and the amount of foreign exchange that was the representation of such gold.

A short history of the gold-exchange standard would show that this system was imposed in India in 1898, the use of gold being reserved for external relations and the use of silver for domestic circulation.

The ingenuity of the system was immediately appreciated, and it spread rapidly to the silver-currency countries—the Philippines in 1903, Mexico in 1905—and, through the mechanism of conversion funds, to countries that had to stay with a paper currency system—Argentina in 1899, Brazil in 1905. Through the operation of the current account of the Treasury, this system also governed the financial relations between some French colonies and their metropolis.

A knowledgeable commentator stated about the gold-exchange standard in 1932: "It affords a quasi colonial and assuredly exotic remedy administered to long-ailing currencies. It is in fact neither a system nor a doctrine, but a makeshift, a rule-of-thumb expedient which is no doubt ingenious, often efficacious, whose flourishing future no one could have suspected at the time."[8]

It was therefore preposterous to interpret the 1922 Genoa Conference resolution recommending the widespread application of the gold-exchange standard as the consequence of a deliberate attempt to improve the monetary system. Even in the minds of its proponents, this widespread application was a mere artificial device, intended to reconcile two conflicting attempts: one aiming at an early restoration of monetary convertibility in the new circumstances arising out of wartime inflationary situations, the other refusing to envisage any possible change in the legal parities between the various currencies.

It was this expedient that received systematic widespread application through the Financial Committee of the League of Nations, which turned it into the basic principle of the monetary system established in all countries whose currencies it rescued: Austria, Hungary, Greece, Bulgaria, Estonia, and the Danzig territory. At the same time, the system was extended to Germany upon the

[8] Edmond Lebée in *Les Doctrines monétaires à l'épreuve des faits* (Paris: Alcan, 1932), p. 137.

recommendation of the Dawes and Young committees, while France agreed to apply it indirectly from 1928 onward with respect to a substantial part of its monetary reserves.

As a result of this generalized extension, the gold-exchange standard had in fact become the monetary system of the West as early as 1925, although France was to adopt it only at a later stage. It was based on two key currencies: the dollar and the pound sterling, together with satellite currencies tied to them in varying degrees.

This was the system that collapsed in 1931 and was engulfed in the catastrophe of the Great Depression.

After the Second World War, in particular when the United States first experienced balance-of-payments difficulties, the gold-exchange standard gradually reemerged, but more insidiously than after the First World War. The moment its principle was accepted, it was viewed with favor by the banks of issue. They thus had the advantage, when they were creditors, of being in a position to substitute interest-bearing assets for the yellow metal that was entirely unproductive, and, when they were debtors, of avoiding the outflow of gold that would have brought their balance-of-payments deficit into full daylight.

There is nothing in the process of the reemergence of the gold-exchange standard that reveals at any juncture, whether in the minds of the heads of state or in those of the governors of the banks of issue, a conscious desire to achieve progress or even an awareness that they were accomplishing a significant act by agreeing to hold foreign currencies among the assets of the central banks.

The extension throughout Europe of the gold-exchange standard between 1922 and 1928, in pursuance of Resolution 9 of the Genoa Conference and under the auspices of the Financial Committee of the League of Nations, was a turning point in history. Although at the time its widespread application seemed to be a purely technical event and remained totally unknown to the general public, it nearly destroyed what we still call Western civilization.

The main impact of the gold-exchange standard was, through the aforementioned duplication phenomenon, to dissociate the evolution of purchasing power from the requirements of economic expansion and to bring it under the unpredictable influences of international capital shifts.

Thus, as a result of capital inflow to Germany, the assets of the Reichsbank increased from 747 million reichsmarks to 1,198 million reichsmarks between 1923 and 1924, and the foreign exchange holdings of the Bank of France rose from 252 million francs to 32,845 million francs from 1927 to 1928.

These huge processes, creating purchasing power without the relevant base, were the one factor that, notwithstanding the offsetting variations that they tended to generate, merrily brought about the worldwide boom of the years 1928–1929 and caused not a general price increase but a spectacular flareup in the prices of stocks and shares in financial markets.

It was obvious, however, that the duplication of purchasing power could not go on indefinitely. In 1931 a collapse occurred, bringing down the foreign-exchange holdings of the Reichsbank from 764 to 120 million reichsmarks between late 1930 and late 1931, those of the Bank of France from 26 to 21 billion francs, and those of Austria from 801 to 140 million shillings.

The collapse of this two-tiered credit structure, to which the gold-exchange standard had given rise, caused a fantastic contraction in purchasing power. This marked the onset of the most formidable deflationary crisis that the world had ever known. Access to foreign markets was becoming impossible; agricultural produce, unsalable. Unemployment was causing havoc in all sectors of the population and was spreading despair and ruin everywhere.

Between 1929 and 1931, the price index fell gradually from 137 to 105 in the United States (base 1928=100), from 124 to 92 in France, from 127 to 89 in Britain, and from 137 to 111 in Germany.

It was evident that, with a change of such magnitude in the nominal value of all wealth, contracts expressed in terms of money could not be fulfilled. Bankruptcy was a common occurrence, and reimbursement of old debts, whether domestic or international, was being suspended throughout the world. At the same time, quota systems, exchange controls, and clearing accounts were being introduced and developed in international trade relations.

The whole network of the legal obligations that are the very stuff of economic life was being unraveled.

Nations reacted in varied ways to this immense catastrophe. The arrangements made to ward it off betokened three different patterns of behavior.

Key-currency countries—in 1930 these were Britain and the United States—had to meet the claims to gold which had been deferred by the introduction of the gold-exchange standard. Strong in their tradition of commercial integrity and observance of contracts, they first attempted to abide by the letter and the spirit of their commitments. Thus, in mid-1931 Britain, whose gold holdings were dwindling, contracted several loans abroad—in particular in France—in order to bolster its foreign-exchange reserves. But, notwithstanding its good intentions, it ultimately had to acknowledge that its efforts were unavailing, and in September or October 1931 had to resign itself to sanctioning the depreciation of sterling, whose price in Paris declined from about 124 francs in 1930 to 89 francs in 1932 and 84 francs in 1933.

This depreciation promptly brought the balance of payments into equilibrium again, and increased the nominal value of the gold holdings by a proportionate amount.

As a result of the choice that it had thus made by accepting a rise for the price of gold comparable to that of other prices, Britain was in a position to restore equilibrium rapidly, eliminate the damage that the gold-exchange standard had caused to the monetary situation, and safeguard the basic principles of its economic and financial civilization.

The United States had a similar experience, although at a later date. It first attempted, like Britain, to uphold and maintain. But in 1933 President Roosevelt decided not only to accept but to effectuate a depreciation of the dollar, i.e., a rise in the price of gold in terms of dollars. The price increased from $20.67 to $35 per ounce in 1934, representing a devaluation of about 69 percent.

This decision by President Roosevelt put an end to the crisis and eliminated the consequences resulting for the United States from the reimbursement of the claims that had so dangerously accumulated under the gold-exchange standard. This grandiose monetary policy saved the United States as it saved the economy of the Western world.

Germany's reactions were in complete contrast with those of Britain and the United States. The banking crisis of 1931 in Germany, where the memory of the major waves of inflation that had come in the wake of the First World War were still very lively, caused a new flight before the mark. An international conference was convened in London in the summer of 1931, under the chairmanship of the Prime Minister, Ramsay MacDonald, in order to seek a remedy. The disrupting influence arose out of the desire of owners of short-term capital invested in Germany to move such capital out of Germany. Their foreign currency demands placed the German balance of payments in jeopardy and forced the Reichsbank to present to the United States and Britain the claims to gold which had accumulated under the gold-exchange standard.

Paradoxically, the remedy was proposed by the Honorable Mr. Stimson, representing the United States. Noting that the danger was due to the tendency of short-term capital to flow out of Germany, he proposed as a remedy that such capital be frozen in the country where it happened to be, notwithstanding the right and desire of the owners to move it out.[9]

The Standstill Committee that was promptly convened in Basel laid down the rules and procedures for the freezing of short-term capital in Germany. By recommending those rules and procedures to the German government, the Committee was unwittingly inventing and installing foreign-exchange controls. In order to maintain the facade of a bygone level of currency behavior, the Committee advised Germany to suspend its foreign commitments and

---

[9] I recounted the proceedings of this ill-fated conference held in London, which I had the honor to attend, in a lecture entitled "Souvenirs et réflexions sur l'age de l'inflation" (Documents du Centre universitaire méditerranéen, 13 February 1956, "Annales du C.U.M.," Vol. IX). This lecture was reproduced in *The Age of Inflation* (Chicago: Regnery, 1964), p. 8.

authorized it to put into effect, with the blessing of its creditors, the system that was to enable Dr. Schacht and Hitler to finance war preparations and finally unleash war itself. Above all, the Committee was sowing the seeds from which inevitably and, so to say, spontaneously would sprout widespread rationing—the basis of the totalitarian civilization that Nazism and Communism were going to champion.

Between these two extremes, other countries—France, Belgium, the Netherlands, and Switzerland—endeavored to maintain their levels of currency behavior, while abiding by their commitments. They formed the "gold bloc," bound together by a common refusal to devaluate, that is, a refusal to change in any way the price of gold in terms of their national currencies.

Their economies sank into a slump and eventually they realized that there were only two alternatives: devaluation, the course adopted by Britain and the United States; or widespread rationing, introduced in Germany and Russia.

In 1936, after serious disturbances, they decided to join the group of countries that had determined to maintain their civilization by sacrificing not their currency, but a legal parity defined by a gold price level which the gold-exchange standard had turned into a mere outdated semblance.

After one or several devaluations, the normal operation of the gold standard restored their economies to prosperity and their balances of payments to equilibrium.

The situation outlined above demonstrates that what went down in the disaster and shame of the Great Depression was not the gold standard but its grotesque caricature in the form of the gold-exchange standard.

To President Roosevelt goes the honor and the glory for having realized in 1934 that if the gold standard was to be a reality again, it was necessary to discard the appearances of a legal parity that the excesses of the gold-exchange standard had deprived of all substance. The "outdated fetish" that he repudiated was not the gold standard, but the monetary level at which it was allowed to operate.

No doubt, the fact that legal parity is pegged is the main feature of the gold standard. I would even say that its major virtue is that it maintains the whole scale of prices in the countries that apply it at a level where the average cost of gold production[10] coincides with the legal parity of the currency. But when its operation has been suspended—as was the case in nearly all belligerent countries during the last two world wars—or disrupted—as was the case as a result of the application in the greater part of the world of a system which, like the gold-exchange standard, stretches nearly to breaking point the link between gold and aggregate purchasing power—then there is no alternative but to jettison appearances to save realities and, while acknowledging the situation that you have allowed to develop, to re-create the basis for continuing expansion without imparing order or stability.

[10] And in the non-gold-producing countries, the average price of gold in terms of exports.

# PART TWO

Attempts at Persuasion

# III

## PRUDENCE AND DISCRETION

The reader will no doubt have noticed that the recommendations made in Chapter I for getting out of the gold-exchange system (see pp. 29–31) are imprecise and ambiguous. They show, however, that the liquidation of the gold-exchange standard will require that very large resources be available, if dollar balances are to be reimbursed. But as regards the procedure whereby such resources can be made available, I have merely suggested two alternatives: the Triffin plan, that is, the creation of money by an appropriate international agency; or an increase in the price of gold.

While suggesting that the first solution would entail inflationary hazards whereas the second one would be efficacious, I did so in cryptic terms, making clear that an increase in the price of gold is by no means certain and that in any case the margin of increase cannot be foreseen.

My obscure wording was deliberate and intentional. I was aware of the possibility that a clear-cut statement regarding the need for an increase in the price of gold could cause speculation that might be dangerous for the reserves of the Bank of France. I was particularly anxious to avoid any inference from the functions that I had previously fulfilled with the Finance Ministry and the Bank of

France, and from the role I had played in the financial "rehabilitation" of 1958, that any solution I advocated was implicity endorsed by the authorities.

Furthermore, I was not unaware of the fact that public opinion in the United States was hostile to any change in the price of gold. I could not therefore hope for any *a priori* decision. The only thing I could wish for was the initiating of a procedure with a view to an objective quest for an efficacious solution. I was certain in my own mind that impartial people would be in favor of a rise in the price of gold if the rationale for such an increase was fully and clearly explained to them. It was this type of mutual enlightenment process that I had in mind when I stated that what had been done by an international conference could be undone only by an international conference (see page 31).

Nevertheless, while at my own behest I was observing a cautious reserve on the delicate matter of the gold price—and continued to do so until such time as the question was brought into full daylight before the general public by General de Gaulle in his resounding press conference of 4 February 1965—I felt it my duty to expound to the French authorities the dangers inherent in the existing international monetary system and the need to bring about its reform before it caused serious disruptions throughout the world, and more specifically in our own country.

On 10 June 1959 I addressed to the Finance Minister a "note concerning some essential reforms":

> Financial rehabilitation is far from complete. Nothing would be more perilous at the present juncture than to rest content in a feeling of complacency and fallacious serenity. This note sets forth some of the reforms that would ward off the serious technical and political dangers threatening the financial rehabilitation we have achieved.
>
> Since convertibility was restored at the end of December last year, the French currency has been pegged to the dollar. Such a step was absolutely necessary, but the

result is that the French price level is tied to the level of prices in the United States. The way in which the claims of American steelworkers are met tomorrow will determine the evolution of the French price index.

Such a situation must not endure. On the other hand, to dissociate the French franc from the dollar would not be either feasible or desirable. The only practicable solution is through closer links between the dollar—and through the dollar, all convertible currencies—and gold.

At present the United States is not prepared to accept such a solution. Yet it is deeply concerned about its gold losses ($2.5 billion during the past year) and feels the long-term dangers that are threatening its currency. The United States is seeking a solution and is prepared to listen to any suggestions and advice.

Now, having achieved financial recovery, we are in a moral position to give guidance and orientation for the restoration of the monetary systems of the West.

If we do not take any initiative in this field, others— probably Germany—will do so. The problem is a complex one, however. I suggest it be studied by a small working party that would be in a position to submit suggestions to the Government in the near future with a view to the establishment of a plan of action.

On 28 February 1961 I addressed myself to this same matter once more in a "note for the Prime Minister":

The economic and financial situation remains sound but calls for decisions in some fields. The dangers that threaten the dollar also threaten the entire Western world with a Great Depression that would certainly result from a collapse of the gold-exchange standard. All the work of financial rehabilitation that has been achieved would be brought into question again.

In my note of 10 June 1959 to the Finance Minister,

I requested that France's attitude, in particular vis-à-vis the United States, be determined. The relevant paragraph read as follows.

(The text of the above-quoted paragraph of my note to the Finance Minister was reproduced here.)

I then concluded:

> President Kennedy's recent message on the United States balance-of-payments position and the financial discussions between the United States and Germany show that such a study is more necessary and urgent than I had thought.

As it seemed that no action was going to be taken in pursuance of my recommendations, I put the matter to General de Gaulle on 16 March 1961. I confirmed my views in a letter which I addressed to him on 5 May 1961:

> Sir,
>
> During the hearing that you were kind enough to grant me on 16 March, you sought my views in particular with respect to the implementation of the reforms which, in accordance with my latest report, could further economic expansion and social progress.
>
> My feeling was that the information I had the honor to submit as regards the monetary situation of the United States had caught your attention. It is my belief that such information might play an important part on the occasion of your forthcoming talks with President Kennedy,[1] in that it would afford the means to represent to him that the situation of the dollar is vulnerable and dangerous and requires support from Western nations, and more specifically from France.
>
> I have just returned from a three-day visit to Wash-

---

[1] President Kennedy was to visit Paris from 31 May to 2 June 1961.

ington. I tried out my arguments on the Chairman of the Federal Reserve Board and on the two Under-secretaries of the Treasury. They could not deny the facts and seemed to be both concerned and surprised at the conclusions to be drawn therefrom.

As regards the dollar crisis, President Kennedy said everything in his message of 6 February 1961, but he did not realize that he was doing so. And to my knowledge no one has ever told him that he had done so.

The current situation is the outcome of a common mistake by the banks of issue of the Western countries when they agreed to substitute for the gold standard a system known as the gold-exchange standard. By accepting this substitution, the banks of issue put themselves in a position of being able to lend immediately to the United States, wholly or in part, the dollars they received in settlement of American balance-of-payments deficits.

What they were in a position to do, many did—in particular, and to a varying degree, the Reichsbank, the Bank of Italy, the Bank of Japan, and the Bank of France.

To the extent that the new system *was* applied, it in fact released the United States from the obligation of settling its foreign debts. Thus the United States was in a position to lend, to give, and even to buy outside its own frontiers without having to worry about its own capacity. Indeed, the United States was able to reap all the benefits of international generosity without immediately experiencing any of the disadvantages.

The situation is summarized by the following figures, taken from President Kennedy's message:

—From 1 January 1951 to 31 December 1960, the cumulative balance-of-payments deficit of the United States was $18.1 billion.

—The gold stock of the United States was $22.8 billion as

of 1 January 1951. On 31 December 1960, the gold
stock would have been reduced to $4.7 billion if at that
time the United States had settled its balance-of-payments deficit.

—Now, on 1 January 1961, the gold holdings of the
United States were still $17.5 billion.

—This apparently strange situation results from the operation of the gold-exchange standard, which has led the
creditor countries to lend $13 billion to the United States
in the form of demand or short-term deposits.

—The present gold holdings of $17.5 billion are currently
saddled with a double liability: the $13 billion of demand
or short-term deposits arising out of the operation of
the gold-exchange standard, and the $11.5 billion re-
quirements necessary under existing regulations for the
backing of domestic circulation in the United States.

The logical conclusion and outcome could be that if
the banks of issue of the Western countries were to take
advantage of the rights that expressly accrue to them as
a result of their demand and short-term deposits, the
Federal Reserve System would be bankrupt tomorrow.
Assuredly they will not do so, at least as long as no
political or merely financial threat induces them to take
such a step for their own safeguard. But it is to be feared
that when such a threat materializes, their sense of duty
toward the currencies that they have to maintain will pre-
vail over their willingness to accommodate the dollar, as
was the case in 1931.

The *de facto* insolvency of the U.S. monetary system
creates grave dangers for the whole of the Western
world, and in particular:

—The threat of a serious dollar crisis, which might jeopardize the hard-won financial stability of all countries holding considerable dollar balances.

—The threat of a major depression, which, *mutatis mutandis*, would be analogous to the Great Depression of the thirties, itself the outcome of the first collapse of the gold-exchange standard.

In an earlier letter to the Finance Minister dated 10 June 1959, I had already suggested that the necessary steps be taken with a view to arranging by joint international action for the salvaging of the dollar. This suggestion was not followed up. It is, however, more justified than ever, considering that the plans now envisaged—to the extent at least that Washington rather than Paris thought it appropriate to inform me—can only prolong for a few months or a few years the mistakes that have brought on the present situation. The action that in 1959 I had hoped would be initiated to arrange the salvaging of the dollar by joint international action is an urgent necessity.

Yet in the present circumstances, France alone is in a position to initiate such action.

It goes without saying that the implementation of my suggestion would require that President Kennedy be apprised of the real situation of the dollar in unequivocal and forceful terms, which until now have been lacking in the exchanges of views to which it has given rise.

If the principle of this change of policy were accepted, I would prepare a memorandum expounding the various aspects of the U.S. monetary situation and bringing out the short-term dangers that it implies not only for the United States but also for all Western countries.[2]

The above memorandum appeared in the form of three articles under the title "The Gold-Exchange Standard: A Danger to the

[2] Reproduction of this letter was specifically authorized by General de Gaulle.

West." I thought that by calling the attention not only of the high authorities concerned but also of the public opinion of several countries that were just as dependent as France upon a reasonable solution to the problem, my arguments would be more forceful. I knew, however, that they would be received with hostility or indifference by the Finance Ministry and the Bank of France.

A letter from the Finance Minister left me in no doubt whatsoever in this respect. On 8 December 1961, in thanking me for the text of "Discours sur le Crédit," a lecture I had just delivered, he wrote to me as follows:

> I am afraid that you have not convinced me on this point. Just as with respect to the gold-exchange standard question, it seems to me that your approach to the problem "suffers from the fact that it is based on the wrong premise." It is not credit policy that is going to resolve the basic problems, and the whole world knows this.

The philosophy on which this remark was based is a well-known one. On several occasions it has given rise to communications from the Governor of the Bank of France to the Finance Minister. It can be summarized as: "The Bank is in no way responsible for the financial difficulties. Let the Government put its own affairs in order, and everything will be all right."

It so happens that since the financial rehabilitation of late 1958, affairs of the state had been in good shape. Yet at the domestic level we had a case of open inflation that was obviously linked to the U.S. balance-of-payments deficit. With budgetary problems resolved for the time being, the problems of credit and of the international monetary system had become, to use the Finance Minister's phrase, "basic problems."

While I had not succeeded in convincing the Finance Minister of the validity of my diagnosis, my views were nevertheless receiving some sympathetic and friendly consideration in circles close to General de Gaulle. The Secretary-General of the Presidency of the Republic, Etienne Burin des Roziers, and I maintained close relations of mutual confidence. This diplomat, later the French Ambassador in Rome, had through unusual and painstaking studies acquired a rare knowledge of financial matters. I knew there was a close community of views between us and was aware that he often mentioned my preoccupations to the President of the Republic.

Furthermore, the Foreign Minister, Maurice Couve de Murville, who had been my immediate colleague when I was Director of the *Mouvement général des Fonds* in the Finance Ministry from 1936 to 1939, held views very close to mine in the financial field. I should think that on more than one occasion he must have called General de Gaulle's attention to the diplomatic implications of the problems arising out of the international monetary system, the continuing U.S. balance-of-payments deficit, and the widespread inflation that it was generating with such dangerous consequences for the creditor countries.

# IV

## GENERAL DE GAULLE'S
## PRESS CONFERENCE

It was on 4 February 1965 that General de Gaulle first took a stand on the need and the role of gold as a basis for international trade. He did so at his press conference on that day, in answering a question concerning foreign investments in France:[1]

"I shall endeavor to make my views on these matters clearly understood. As the states of Western Europe, decimated and ruined by wars, are regaining their substance, the comparative status to which their weakening had led appears improper, excessive, and dangerous. This finding does not imply on their part—and in particular on the part of France—anything inimical to other countries, in particular the United States. Indeed, the fact that such states are increasingly desirous of having full freedom of action on anything that pertains to international relations is simply inherent in the changing nature of things. This is the case as regards the monetary relationships that have prevailed throughout the world ever since the days when Europe's ordeals destroyed its equilibrium. I

[1] The text reproduced here is taken from *Discours et messages* (Plon, 1970), Vol. IV, pp. 330 ff. Reproduction was expressly authorized by General de Gaulle.

am referring, as surely everybody realizes, to the system that emerged shortly after the end of the First World War and was reestablished after the Second World War.

"It is common knowledge that, as a result of the Genoa Conference in 1922, this system had conferred upon two currencies, the pound and the dollar, the privilege of being automatically regarded as equivalent to gold for all international payments purposes. Other currencies were not so regarded. Later on, as the pound was devalued in 1931 and the dollar in 1933, it looked as if this major advantage was in jeopardy. But the United States came out of the Great Depression. Then the Second World War ruined European currencies by unleashing inflation. Now nearly all the gold reserves in the world were in the hands of the United States, which being supplier to the whole world had maintained the value of its national currency. Therefore it could seem natural that other states should include dollars or gold, indifferently, in their foreign-exchange reserves, and that balance-of-payments equilibrium should be achieved by transferring U.S. credit or currency as well as gold. The more so as the United States had no difficulty in settling its debts with gold if requested to do so. This international monetary system, the so-called gold-exchange standard, thus became common practice.

"Today, however, it seems that this system no longer tallies with the facts, and therefore its drawbacks are becoming increasingly burdensome. The problem can be examined in an adequate spirit of serenity and objectivity because there is nothing very urgent or very alarming in the present situation and the present juncture is therefore propitious for such an examination.

"The circumstances that led to the gold-exchange standard in the past are indeed different now. The currencies of Western nations have been rehabilitated, so much so that the total gold reserves of the Six are now equal to those of the United States. They would be even higher if the Six determined to convert all their dollar holdings into gold. It is therefore clear that the convention under which the dollar is an international currency of transcendent value no longer rests on the initial basis, which was that the United States owned the major part of the world's gold. But there is more. The fact that many countries as a matter of principle accept dollars as well as gold to offset the U.S. balance-of-payments deficits leads to a situation wherein the United States is heavily in debt without having to pay. Indeed, what the United States owes to foreign countries it pays—at least in part—with dollars that it can simply issue if it chooses to. It does so instead of paying fully with gold whose value is real, which one owns only because one has earned it, and which cannot be transferred to other countries without any danger or any sacrifice. This unilateral facility that is available to the United States contributes to the gradual disappearance of the idea that the dollar is an impartial and international trade medium, whereas it is in fact a credit instrument reserved for one state only.

"Actually such a situation carries other consequences. In particular, the United States is under no obligation to settle its payments deficits in gold—at least not for the full amount—as was the case formerly under the old rule, which required states to take adequate—and sometimes stringent—steps to correct their disequilibrium. The result is that year after year they run a balance-of-payments deficit. Not that they run an adverse trade balance. Far from it! Their physical exports are always in excess of their physical imports. But such is also the case with their dollar outflows, which are in excess of the dollar inflows. In other words, as a result of a process known by the name of inflation, huge amounts of money are created in the United States and subsequently exported overseas in the form of dollar loans extended to foreign countries or private individuals. In view of the fact that in the United States this generates an increase in the total credit proxy, so that investments at home are less remunerative, there emerges in the United States an increasing propensity to invest overseas. Hence, in some countries, some sort of expropriation of a number of undertakings.

"There is no doubt that this practice considerably favored and still favors to some extent the multiple and considerable assistance which the United States is extending to many countries to further their development and from which we ourselves benefited abundantly in the past.[2] But circumstances today are such that one can even wonder how serious a disturbance there would be if all countries holding dollars came to request, sooner or later, conversion into gold. Even though such a widespread move may never come to pass, it is a fact that there is, so to speak, a fundamental disequilibrium.

"For all these reasons, France recommends that the system be changed. This is what it did in particular on the occasion of the monetary conference held in Tokyo.[3] Considering that a crisis occurring in this field would probably shatter the whole world, we have every reason to wish that every step be taken in due time to avoid it. We consider that international exchanges must be established, as was the case before the great worldwide disasters, on an unquestionable monetary basis that does not bear the mark of any individual country.

"What basis? Actually, it is difficult to envision in this regard any other criterion, any other standard than gold. Yes, gold, which does not change in nature, which can be made either into bars, ingots, or coins, which has no nationality, which is considered, in all places and at all times, the immutable and fiduciary value par excellence. Furthermore, despite all that it was possible to imagine, say, write, or do in the midst of major events, it is a fact that even today no currency has any value except by direct or indirect relation to gold, real or supposed. Doubtless, no one would think of dictating to any country how to manage its domestic affairs. But the supreme law, the golden rule—and indeed it is pertinent to say it—which must be enforced and honored again in international economic relations, is the duty to balance, from one monetary area

[2] Through the Marshall Plan, which from late 1947 onward contributed greatly to the rehabilitation of European economies after the Second World War.
[3] The annual meeting of the International Monetary Fund, held in Tokyo, September 1964. France's monetary views, presented by Valéry Giscard-d'Estaing, the Finance Minister, were strongly criticized in a press conference by Douglas Dillon, U.S. Secretary of the Treasury.

to another, by effective inflows and outflows of gold, the balance of payments resulting from their exchanges.

"Naturally, the smooth termination of the gold-exchange standard, the restoration of the gold standard, and supplemental and interim measures that might be called for, in particular with a view to organizing international credit on this new basis, will have to be deliberately agreed upon between countries, in particular those on which there devolves special responsibility by virtue of their economic and financial capabilities. In fact we already have the necessary framework for the normal conduct of such studies and negotiations. The International Monetary Fund, which was established in order to ensure solidarity between the various currencies to the greatest extent possible, could provide an appropriate forum for all countries, if the question was no longer to perpetuate the gold-exchange standard, but to replace it. The Group of Ten, which, in addition to the United States and Britain, comprises on the one hand France, Germany, Italy, the Netherlands, and Belgium and, on the other hand, Japan, Sweden, and Canada, could draw up the necessary proposals. Lastly, it could be a matter for the Six, which seem to be on the way to achieving a European Economic Community, to establish between themselves and to vindicate abroad the sound system that common sense advocates and that is consonant with the reviving power of our old Continent.

"France, for its part, is prepared to participate actively in the reform that the interest of the whole world demands."

# V

---

## INTERVIEW WITH
## *THE ECONOMIST*


The day after the resounding statement by General de Gaulle, *The Economist* of London requested me to grant an interview on "The Role and the Rule of Gold." This major British periodical offered to send to Paris its distinguished Assistant Editor, Fred Hirsch, and to reproduce in full a recording of our talk.

The text was published in *The Economist*[1] and subsequently in a pamphlet issued by Princeton University, under the auspices of Professor Machlup of the International Finance Section.[2]

As this conversation afforded me an opportunity to expound my views on quite a number of points, it is reproduced here. However, I would urge the reader to bear in mind that this is not a systematic statement, but a mere rambling exchange of views on items of major topical interest.

In the text that follows, my *Economist* interviewer is designated by his initials, F.H., and I by the initials J.R.

---

[1] "Return to Gold—Argument with Jacques Rueff," 13 February 1965.
[2] No. 47, dated June 1965, entitled "The Role and the Rule of Gold."

## THE ROLE AND THE RULE OF GOLD:
## AN EXCHANGE OF VIEWS

F.H. M. Rueff, you are a man, to say the least, of distinctive ideas, and most people, ourselves included, have hitherto dismissed your ideas on a return to the gold standard as irrelevant nostalgia. Yet now, as one commentator has put it, we see you as scriptwriter to General de Gaulle. How do you get your ideas across?

J.R. Well, first I must protest against this notion. I am not in any degree scriptwriter to General de Gaulle. You see, General de Gaulle does not need a scriptwriter. Still more: I have no responsibility at all in the wording of his last message and I do not know anybody who has any such responsibility; he did it absolutely alone. It is true that I have had many opportunities since the financial reform of 1958 to express my views, and my concern about the gold-exchange standard is a very old one. As early as 16 March 1961 I made clear to him that we had more or less stabilized the franc in terms of the dollar and that we were strongly interested in the stability and the solvency of the dollar itself. And therefore, that we had not only the right, but the duty to see that there was no danger in the money standard that was the base of our own money. My only influence has been to express my view in the most candid way, through my notes to and talks with the authorities concerned.

F.H. Do you see yourself, in exerting this general influence, as in any rivalry with the official advisers in the Bank of France and the Ministry of Finance?

J.R. Well, they are all friends of mine. I have served many years both in the Treasury and on the board of the Bank of France; I do not think there is any question of rivalry. There may be a different tendency. Well, there is no doubt that there has been some difference of inspiration. But the trend is changing quite a lot.

F.H. The official trend?

J.R. The general trend in the world. If we look at the wind from the east, it is teaching some principles on the role of the price mechanism and of profits which are very valuable for us. And if we look at what has happened in Germany in the realm of the *Soziale Marktwirtschaft*, we see a policy, basically established on market forces, corrected with social inspiration that tends to make it acceptable even politically for the people. We have more or less the same trend in France. I am sometimes considered a survival of the past. . . . Many times I feel bold enough to consider myself a precursor of the future.

F.H. That's interestingly put. But may I ask you this? You have a very respected intellectual position in France; you are a member of the Académie Française. But within your own discipline, among economists, you are relatively isolated, especially in your international ideas. Do you feel at all worried about this?

J.R. You said I am a member of the French Academy. I have the great privilege of being the successor of a poet, Jean Cocteau. And he said somewhere that to be influential you have to be dead. *Il faut être un homme vivant, mais un auteur posthume.* Well, of course, as long as you are alive there are always some objections; but I remember the teaching of my predecessor and I hope that my posthumous influence may be effective.

And I am not so sure that I am isolated. For instance, in my second committee in 1960 on the obstacles to economic expansion, I had with me about sixty rapporteurs who were all the young people in the administration, and we felt extraordinarily united. And don't forget that my report was unanimously approved even by the representatives of the three noncommunist trade unions. Of course, there has been a lot of divergence about my views; but may I say that in the end they have always been adopted—which doesn't suggest any isolation!

F.H. I meant on the international-gold-standard side. Could you perhaps tell us now your particular objections to the gold-exchange standard and why in particular you think that it should be replaced, not as people like Triffin and we ourselves

believe, by an increase in international credit, but rather by a
return to gold itself?

J.R. I wrote in 1961 that the West was risking a credit collapse
and that the gold-exchange standard was a great danger for
Western civilization. If I did so, it is because I am convinced
—and I am very emphatic on this point—that the gold-
exchange standard attains to such a degree of absurdity that
no human brain having the power to reason can defend it.
What is the essence of the system, and what is its difference
from the gold standard? It is that when a country with a key
currency runs a balance-of-payments deficit—that is to say,
the United States, for example—it pays the creditor country
dollars, which end up with the latter's central bank. But the
dollars are of no use in Bonn or in Tokyo or in Paris. The
very same day, they are reloaned to the New York money
market, so that they return to the place of origin. Thus the
debtor country does not lose what the creditor country has
gained. So the key-currency country never feels the effect of
a deficit in its balance of payments. And the main consequence
is that there is no reason whatever for the deficit to disappear,
because it does not appear.

Let me be more positive: If I had an agreement with my tailor
that whatever money I pay him he returns to me the very
same day as a loan, I would have no objection at all to order-
ing more suits from him and my own balance of payments
would then be in deficit.

F.H. But isn't this to some extent in the nature of all credit? After
all, I deposit money in a bank and the bank will lend the
money to somebody else—possibly even somebody connected
with me. Isn't your objection to this international use of credit
really an objection to the internationalization of what is in the
nature of all credit?

J.R. I don't think I agree with this presentation. Of course, you
could say that what the gold-exchange standard does not do,
that is, contract global demand in the debtor country, could
be done by deliberate credit policy.

F.H. Yes.

J.R. Theoretically it seems possible. But let us first realize that, if any country in the world had been in a position to do that, it would be the United States. It has in government employ more economists, and I think more readers of *The Economist,* than any other country in the world. And it has had for five years an enormous deficit in its balance of payments. If it has not done by deliberate credit policy what the gold standard would have done by automatically restricting purchasing power, it is proof that it is not possible. And why is it not possible? I cannot imagine any parliamentary country with a democratic regime in which you could do such a difficult thing.

F.H. Except under stress.

J.R. Even under stress. A policy that restricts aggregate demand is feasible only to the extent that it is pursued automatically, day after day, and that its hardly perceptible effects are not felt by anybody.

F.H. Many of us largely agree with your criticisms of the gold-exchange standard, which interestingly are much the same kind of criticisms as are made from the other wing by Triffin. But what I cannot understand in your proposed solution to return to gold is this. Suppose, for example, that the United States had taken your advice in 1961 and had then trebled the price of gold, to $100 an ounce. Would it not now, with so much larger a gold reserve in relation to its liabilities, feel able, in fact, to continue its balance-of-payments deficit for much *longer?*

J.R. Well, this point must be taken in detail. You have first named my friend Triffin. I must say that we are in full agreement on the diagnosis. We differ on the remedy, but the diagnosis is the same. You have spoken of trebling the price of gold in 1961. I consider the price of gold as only a side issue. It is not at all the aim; it is not at all a remedy; rather it is only a small condition of which I shall speak later. The aim is to restore a system which is not contrary to the most elementary common sense, in other words, to ensure that the debtor country loses what the creditor country gains.

And let us be more specific on this point. It needs no economic theory to identify the main reason for the deficit of the U.S. balance of payments: it is that despite all the past deficits there has never been any scarcity of money in the New York money market.[3] Why? Because the dollars that are paid out are immediately returned to the New York money market and are always available there for further investment, at home or abroad.

We sometimes complain of the excessive invasion of foreign interests in Europe. Personally, I am not afraid of that. The cause is not at all a desire of the United States to conquer Europe. The cause is that the creditor countries themselves have created the situation that makes it possible and automatic for the United States to invest abroad, because there is always so much excess liquidity in the New York money market. It has to find an outlet.

F.H. You are referring here to the flow of Eurodollars back to New York?

J.R. I am referring to the simple mechanism of the gold-exchange standard which involves that, when a central bank receives dollars, it returns them the very same day by wire, say, through the purchase of Treasury bills in the New York market, or a bank deposit.

F.H. But may one try to pin you down on this? I accept that in principle an increase in the gold price may not be your *aim*, but, nevertheless, if it is part of the *means*, we do have to consider what the result would be.

J.R. I have until now always avoided speaking about the price of gold explicitly, because I did not want to create difficulty for the central banks or to engender speculation in gold. But now

---

[3] This statement was made in 1965. The situation is different in 1972.

the question is in the open and there is no reason to keep the same discretion.

The price of gold is to me incidental; what I want to restore is the rule of the gold standard. That means that from the date of the reform the central banks will return to the old rule, of creating money only against gold or bills in national currency. In other words, they shall not build up, except for daily settlement, any assets in dollars. Well, from that moment on, I am entirely convinced, the deficit of the balance of payments of the United States will disappear in less than three months. This is a very audacious prediction. But I have never seen a country with a system of international payments involving real transfers of purchasing power in which the deficit stayed more than three months after it had reestablished the balance between aggregate demand and the aggregate value of all the wealth offered for sale in the market. I mean, after it has eliminated the inflationary surplus. So, what I really have in mind is to restore a system conducive to such equilibrium.

But then there appears the side issue—and purely a side issue—which is the liquidation of the past. We have accumulated such large dollar balances (i.e., sight-claims to U.S. gold) that we can only come back to the free operation of a transfer mechanism, involving the possibility for non-American holders of dollars to secure free conversion thereof into gold, when U.S. currency is no longer under the menace of these balances and of the insolvency they may bring.

Therefore, they must either be funded or reimbursed. The funding would be very difficult to obtain and would do great harm.

F.H. It would be very deflationary; and you say you are not a deflationist!

J.R. Most certainly not. I will come back to that. Well, for the reimbursement you have two solutions, you have an option. One is the Triffin plan to entrust the IMF with the task of meeting requests for the reimbursement of dollar balances by creating money; the other is an increase in the price of gold. All the other plans are in between; and these are the two families of remedies.

F.H. Yes.

J.R. Well, the Triffin plan is typical of one of these two families. I do not like it because I think it will give a monetary or a fiscal authority the power to decide the amount of credit that ought to be created. I myself have acted for a monetary authority for many months, and I know that these authorities are not able, they have not the power—the human possibility, at least in our regime—to follow the policy they ought to. I repeat, if it were possible, the Federal Reserve Board—probably intellectually the loftiest organization in the field of money—would have done it. But they have done just the reverse: you see that they have always compensated the outflow of gold by creation of new credit. I do not mean to say that they have done it intentionally.

F.H. Why not? They do after all follow a conscious, managed credit policy and not an automatic one. Surely they do not claim and they do not want, and ought not to want, blindly to follow an automatic policy?

J.R. I am not sure that you are right. Let me tell you that my friends in Washington told me in 1962 that I was wrong in thinking that the deficit of the balance of payments in the United States would survive as long as the gold-exchange standard survived. They told me they had a timetable according to which the deficit would be reduced by one-half at the end of 1962, and disappear at the end of 1963. But it did not; it could not, because the very essence of the gold-exchange standard is to maintain the deficit of reserve currency countries. As long as the deficit is not automatically felt in the credit structure of the debtor country, the deficit goes on. So I do not hesitate to forecast the future. I am absolutely *convinced* that the deficit of the balance of payments of the

United States will not disappear as long as we maintain the gold-exchange standard. And in 1962 I backed this forecast with a rash bet with one of my Washington friends: a bet of one dollar a year.

F.H. Gold-guaranteed, I trust?

J.R. Not gold-guaranteed.

F.H. You say, and many people will instinctively agree, that you don't believe that any human management could be so all-knowing as to manage credit correctly in exactly the right way. But the objection many people have to your preference for the gold standard as such is that this would leave the volume of credit not, as now, in the imperfect hands of the best central-banking authorities we have, but rather in the completely arbitrary hands of the goldmining companies of South Africa, the trading policy of the Communist Party of the Soviet Union, or whatever technical discoveries happen to be made that might increase or decrease the world's credit base by quite wild amounts, in a way that not even the stupidest monetary authority would do.

J.R. But it was not I, it was first Adam Smith and then Keynes, in his last letter, who spoke of the "invisible hand" that results from the price mechanism. Credit management is not stupid, as such. But it very often is stupid when it is done in the wrong direction, so as, for instance, to compensate for the internal consequences of the gold movement. I fully accept the conscious use of the discount rate and of open-market policy—provided it tends to bring about the market situation that would have resulted from the gold movements and does not systematically reverse it.

F.R. Are you in favor of the pre-1931 gold standard, where all parities were constantly stable?

J.R. I am not in favor of floating exchange rates. I am not in favor of daily changes of parity. But when you have had very exceptional situations you may need exceptional policies to clean up the past. Let us take a positive example. It is what President Franklin D. Roosevelt did in raising the price of gold in 1934—and I would like my friends in Washington to keep that in mind.

It is often said that what we want to avoid is the return of the trouble and the mischief of the gold standard in the twenties. But if you take the balance sheets of the central banks you will see that the mischief was not the mischief of the gold standard but the mischief of the gold-exchange standard. The evolution of the balance sheets of the central banks is exactly the same, exactly parallel in the years 1927, 1928, and 1929 to what it is now, and it is the collapse of this system in 1931 that was responsible for the depth of the depression.

F.H. But one of the countries that saw the biggest constriction imposed by the gold standard was, of course, Britain—which held no foreign exchange in its reserves. And, as we have always recognized, Britain at this time suffered precisely *because* of the harsh and inflexible disciplines of the gold standard, which you now want to restore.

J.R. Let me tell you that you touch a point on which I have quite a few personal recollections. In 1930 I was financial attaché in the French Embassy in London, and in that capacity I was responsible for the deposits of the French Treasury with British banks. They were the direct result of eight years of the gold-exchange standard, because we had kept the pounds sterling in London, as my colleagues in New York had kept in the American market the dollars that had been pouring into the French Treasury from 1927 onward. Then, in 1931, the failure of the Austrian Creditanstalt caused successive waves of repatriations; and it was this collapse of the gold-exchange standard that, without any possible doubt, transformed the depression of 1929 into the Great Depression of 1931.

F.H. While you are on this historical episode, what would your comments be on the very widespread view that it was to a substantial extent French pressure on London at that time, through the withdrawal of sterling balances, that was in part responsible for the general collapse later on?

J.R. Let me tell you that, unhappily for the world, the French pressure did not exist, or was so mild that it had no effect. There is a very interesting document from this period, a letter from Sir Austen Chamberlain, who was then Foreign Secretary in London, to M. Poincaré, who was Prime Minister and Finance Minister in France; it must be of 1928. Sir Austen said, "We know that you are entitled to ask gold for your sterling, but in the frame of the close friendship between Britain and France we ask you, so as to avoid trouble for the City of London, not to do that." And we were, I must say, weak enough to comply with this request and not ask for gold. The fact that I had such important sterling deposits in London shows that we did not use this right to ask for gold. The adjustment, which would hardly have been felt if carried out on a day-to-day basis, was not made, and we had the fantastic boom of 1927, 1928, and 1929. This explains the depth of the collapse and of the depression, because the adjustment was so long delayed. We were too gentle in complying with official appeals not to convert our sterling balances into gold.

It is exactly the position in which we are now. We are moving without any doubt to the same kind of outcome as in 1931, because it is so clear that the dollar is approaching the end of its acceptability for payment abroad, and we shall have the same disruption of the existing system.[4] But in delaying it through various devices—by the increase of the quotas of the International Monetary Fund, the Roosa bonds, the central-banking swap credits, the Basel agreement, the agreement of the Group of Ten, and all the rest—we are doing exactly the same thing, namely, delaying the correction of the U.S. balance-of-payments deficit. If we acted as genuine friends of our friends, we should do exactly the reverse.

F.H. But would you not say, M. Rueff, that the very developments that you cite—first the Basel agreement, then the growing agreement among even some Continental central banks on the

[4] This disruption occurred on 17 March 1968.

need to replace dollar and sterling liquidity by an expansion of assets in the International Monetary Fund—that this very movement is itself an indication that a return to the crude gold base as such is not necessary and that the threat of another 1931 is, or ought to be, now an entirely artificial threat? It is artificial to the extent that there is a certain movement toward the creation of some kind of international credit management, which many people, starting from Keynes, have seen as the only logical development of credit management on a national scale.

J.R. Well, your question has two sides. I would be in full agreement with you if I could believe that this process of avoiding the facts could go on long enough; in other words, that we could maintain indefinitely, for instance, what we did in 1928–1929: not asking for gold in London. But do you not see clearly that the dollar is very near the limit of its payment abroad? Look at the figures. The gold stock in the United States is diminishing by a billion dollars every year and the claim on gold increasing two billion dollars every year. Of course you can release some gold by lowering or abolishing the gold reserve requirement for the internal currency. I have no objection to that, because the present percentage of cover is purely arbitrary. But the situation, if it continues—and it will continue, that is the basis of my reasoning—is bound to come to a point where there will be no foreign exchange left and no gold left to pay abroad. I know this situation very well. In 1958, when I had to look at the French situation, we had no foreign exchange at all left in the Equalization Fund. We were informed by the United States—and they were quite right, they acted as very good friends when they told us, "We will not give you any more money as long as you do not improve your situation." I was and am very grateful for this. I knew at the time that we were quite unable to pay anything abroad and the only option was either to establish quotas on every import (which we did) and to restrict foreign travel (which we did), or to improve the underlying situation (which we did a little later). Well, don't you see that the situation in the United States is exactly the same, *mutatis mutandis*? They are now discussing, in Washington, a tax of a hundred dollars on the people who want to go abroad.

To conclude on this point, I would say that I would agree with you if I were not convinced that we are in the position of a man who falls from the fifth floor. As long as he is falling, all is well, but he is sure, absolutely sure, to crash to the ground. And when he reaches the ground, the situation will not be comfortable. And that's what I want to avoid, our hitting the floor.

But that leads to the second point. You consider that any reform along my lines would mean a great deflation.

F.H. I would say I am very worried that it would lead to a great deflation. But one's concern is not only that. One's real concern is that it would lead to a completely arbitrary influence over international economic policy—that your system would always be arbitrary and would be in danger of being deflationary.

J.R. Well, let me refer again to what President Roosevelt did in 1934. Roosevelt did not destroy the gold standard, he restored it. Of course, it was a special kind of gold standard only for central banks, but I am very satisfied with that; but he definitely restored the gold standard through an increase in the price of gold.

Well, what would happen if we tried to do the same thing today? We know that prices in the United States have doubled since 1934. So, suppose we roughly double the price of gold; the amount of the gold stock of the United States, which is now approximately $15 billion, would then be $30 billion. Meanwhile the claims on this gold from the central banks would not change: they are, generally speaking, not claims with a gold clause, they are claims in dollars. I must insist that the central banks have no right whatever to claim fixed quantities of gold, you cannot presume a gold clause where it is not expressed.

F.H. Some central banks do presume it, *de facto*.

J.R. I have much to say about that. I have been a judge in the European Court for ten years. If you make a loan without a gold clause, you are supposed to know what you are doing. Therefore, with these $30 billion the United States could repay the $13 billion of claims of the central banks, and the United States would be left with $17 billion of gold, which is a little more than it has now.[5] Therefore, there would be no change whatever in the position with respect to credit in the United States.

With respect to the creditor central banks, their dollar claims would have been repaid and replaced by an amount of gold having the same value on the basis of the new gold price. So here too there would be no change. And let me tell you that if there were no journalists in the world, nobody would even notice the change.

But I must insist on one essential point. I consider it a crime against order and stability to speak of a change in the price of gold without speaking of the reimbursement of the dollar claims, because the change in the price of gold has no other justification. It is only the means to liquidate a situation which is the result of our past errors.

F.H. But what guarantee would you have that, after this increase in the price of gold and without any conscious international credit arrangements, you would not get precisely the same gold-exchange standard evolving again? I know all about the Genoa Conference and its resolutions in 1922. But after 1934, I believe, there was no specific intention of re-creating the gold-exchange standard, it just happened.

J.R. You are quite right.

F.H. And surely this will always just happen, because gold is in practice a poor, barren asset, bearing no interest. And central

---

[5] This computation was based on the amount of dollar balances existing in 1965. Claims denominated in dollars having increased in the meantime, the conclusions derived now would be substantially different.

banks can and do find income-producing employment for their reserves.

J.R. Well, you are to remember that they are nonprofit organizations.

F.H. May I come now to practicalities? Whatever you or anyone else may want, it is very clear that the United States has elevated to a position of high political policy the maintenance of the gold price at $35 an ounce. Now in this situation, in your opinion, what degree of pressure ought to be exerted by countries or central banks that think otherwise? Do you think, for example, in the light of what you were saying about 1931, that France and other European countries ought now to be tougher about converting dollar balances into gold?

J.R. I am a great believer in human reason, and I consider that when a thing is clear to me it can be made clear to other people, if they are in good faith and provided the question is discussed. But for five years the question has not been discussed. The Group of Ten were confined to a very narrow field for their studies of the problem. They were forbidden to discuss a change in the price of gold, and therefore the main solution is closed to them. And then they commit a serious mistake by agreeing to call lack of "liquidity" what is really lack of "dollars." You know the story of the monk who wanted to eat meat on Friday; he said to the rabbit, "I baptize you a carp." Well, we have called lack of liquidity what is really lack of dollars, and we have really lost three years in discussing questions which are not real.

F.H. But given this, what degree of pressure?

J.R. Well, the pressure must be for an invitation to discuss the question openly and frankly with us.

If it appears that there is no hope whatever of getting people to agree to a common solution that seems reasonable, it may happen, and it probably will, that each country will defend its own interest. But I refuse to accept this hypothesis. Before deciding whether pressure is required, we have first to see whether it is not a matter for intellectual discussion.

F.H. But surely this intellectual discussion is happening in the Ossola Committee and the Paris Club?

J.R. No. For as long as you call what is really the problem of the gold-exchange standard a problem of liquidity, there is no discussion of the real problem. I have nowhere seen a recommendation for the reimbursement of the dollar balances. As long as you do not approach this point you have no discussion. And I am convinced that when the problem has been clearly and fully stated it will be possible to arrive at an agreement. The question is whether it will be done before or after the crisis.

F.H. Might I move now, M. Rueff, to one remark of the General's last week with which I am sure you would be in agreement? This was where he stated that a national currency has a value only in relation to gold. Now many of us would almost put it the other way around, and say that gold has a value, a real value, only in relation to a national currency.

J.R. Let me tell you that I have not at all any religious belief in gold. Gold is not at all an aim, it is only a means for a certain policy.

F.H. In effect what you are saying is that you prefer the anonymous, and we would say arbitrary, discipline of gold to the conscious discipline of men—of credit-controllers, international credit-controllers.

J.R. I accept anonymous, I do not accept arbitrary; because it is not at all arbitrary, since it is based on the real facts and objective needs.

F.H. But surely arbitrary in this sense: I believe that last year gold production was less than $1.5 billion. Suppose that for technical reasons, because of some new discovery in Siberia or some quite local technical development in South Africa, the production of gold in the world in 1966 is not $1.5 billion but $6 billion. Now is not that an arbitrary influence on the amount of international means of payment available?

J.R. Yes, I agree on one point. If you have a sudden lack of continuity, I would have no objection to a change, in these exceptional circumstances which you envisage, in the price of gold.

F.H. The price of gold should then change in relation to its supply?

J.R. Yes, but simultaneously in all convertible-currency countries.

F.H. But this change would itself require a conscious decision of credit management, in no way different from what you are saying is so difficult.

J.R. Not at all, not at all. It would be a rare, quite exceptional move.

F.H. But if, in line with your ideas, gold were to be the only means of international settlement, are you not worried that there might be insufficient means of international payment, given the fact that in the last two years, as both you and Professor Triffin have so clearly shown, gold has constituted only quite a small fraction of the increase in international liquidity?

J.R. Yes, but this fraction is as small as the degree of stability in the world.[6] Do not forget that in all countries that are not key-currency countries, we now have stabilization plans, income policies, and other efforts to counter the inflationary effect of the excessive increase in liquidity.

F.H. So, in other words, you do see the return to gold as one of the means of imposing a much greater discipline over credit expansion, in particular domestic credit expansion, than we have had in recent years?

J.R. I think that internal credit expansion has not been the main fault of the system. The main fault has been the result of the gold-exchange standard, and if we restore a real system of payments internationally I think that would leave *more* freedom for internal policy.

---

[6] J.R. uses this terse formula to show that monetary instability and more particularly price instability have never been so great as since the introduction into international liquidity of an increasing proportion of non-metallic assets, i.e., dollar balances and all subsequent related modalities.

F.H. But, if I may say so M. Rueff, this is where I, and I think other people, get very mixed up about the real aims of your scheme.

On the one side you can say, and there many conservative banking authorities will tend to agree, that a return to the gold standard would impose greater domestic discipline and prevent the inflationary pressures that, as they see it, we have been having recently.

But one can also put it quite differently—and I am quite unclear which of these two positions you are taking—one can also say quite differently that in practice, as in 1934, a big increase in the price of gold would give more freedom to domestic credit management simply because of the great increase in external financial strength, in particular of the United States. And that it would in this way, at least in its first consequences, remove a discipline that we have had already.

I think, if many people reject the sovereign rule of gold, it is just because it is so arbitrary in the sense reflected here, in these two possibly quite different effects. It could be intensely deflationary; and, equally, it could be highly inflationary.

J.R. I think there is a misunderstanding in the meaning of discipline. I think what you imply by discipline is a kind of conscious action which will be generated by movement of gold as an alarm clock. That is not what I have in mind. If I want the gold standard, it is not because it will impose on central banks a certain policy. It is because it will exert its own influence by the transfer of purchasing power which is the result of the transfer of gold.[7]

F.H. That seems an extraordinarily mechanistic view. But, coming

---

[7] This statement is made more explicit in my paper entitled "Elements for a Theory of the Discount Rate and the Balance of Payments" (*Revue Economique*, July 1957), which was reproduced in full in *Balance of Payments* (New York: Macmillan, 1967), p. 179.

now to more immediate things: if you had to select a date for your guess as to when an increase in the price of gold, which you see as inevitable, will come, what would be your guess?

J.R. Well, let me remind you that the Oracle of Delphi never gave a date for its forecast. What I am sure of is that, if we continue to operate under the same system, we shall some day arrive at the end of the means of external payments by the United States. This will mean that, whether it wants to or not, whatever the agreement in the IMF and the GATT, the United States will have to establish an embargo on gold, establish quotas on imports, and impose restrictions such as the one it is now studying on foreign travel, thereby gravely affecting the links between nations.[8] I know the situation so well because many times in my career I have seen the same situation in France.

F.H. But the United States is today the only country that officially gives other countries the facility to exchange its currency into gold at an official rate. Now, what do you think would happen to the price of gold if the Federal Reserve, together perhaps with a number of other like-minded central banks, were to say it would refuse to *buy* gold at $35—or at any price whatsoever? What would then happen, do you believe, to the price of gold?

J.R. The price of gold would fall to a very low level and nothing would make it possible to maintain it. Unless, of course, there were great speculation which convinced people that gold was still a refuge. But one cannot forecast. I fully agree with you, the price of gold is not in itself something given by God, it's the result of a policy.

F.H. Do you believe that General de Gaulle realizes this?

J.R. He has shown that he is fully informed of the mysteries of the gold standard and the gold-exchange standard. For my-

---

[8] So many steps which, with the exception of the first one, were specifically spelled out in the San Antonio address of 1 January 1968 (see further, page 153).

self, I feel that the proposition that the IMF or the Committee of Ten or any institution of this kind should receive the free disposition of an important part of the gold reserves of a country is not realistic at all. Would your country agree to transfer—either to Basel or to the European community or to whatever body—the disposal of its gold reserve?

F.H. Disposal of its gold reserves, no. I would just say that in my experience countries give up just as much power to the international institutions as they have to; but under pressure it is surprising what may be done. The point I was trying to make, though, is simply that, as is perhaps not generally enough realized, the United States does today have this quite singular and unique function of maintaining dollar-gold convertibility. If in practice the United States ceased to do this, such as by saying it would not buy gold at any price, I think we might come to the point where somebody else would have to pick up the job, and perhaps only an international organization could.

J.R. I am not interested in the price of gold. If you want to replace gold by something better, platinum or any other metal, as I told you, I have no religious belief in gold. It is only an instrument; it has been in the past less bad than the others, that is all we can say.

F.H. But you do not think that the present tendency of countries to want to hold gold as distinct from dollars—I am thinking in particular of France here—might be rather different if the countries thought that there was a possibility that the price of gold might fall as well as rise? And that it was not gold as such, in General de Gaulle's terms, that had an intrinsic value that would last for ever more? Insofar as this attitude is not quite correct, which you admit now, is not the faith in gold as an instrument of reserve also slightly dubious?

J.R. I do not think there is any idea of speculation in the mind of General de Gaulle. I think he is convinced that the problem for the West is to replace an instrument of disorder with an instrument tending to restore order, and this is what he has in mind. I think there are very few people who consider it realistic under present conditions that gold should be abandoned.

F.H. Let us hope there will be more after Thursday[9] last.

Might I move now to a more technical point? What is your view of what is here called the CRU, the Composite Reserve Unit?

J.R. It is difficult for me to express a view, because I do not know much about the details of this scheme. It has been proposed, I know, by my friend the French Finance Minister, and I think it is up to him to defend his own child. It seems to me that it is a scheme of the family either of the European Payments Union or even the IMF. Generally speaking, I think that anything can be done in this field, provided it is built on the basis of money-gold convertibility. The CRU system can be good or it can be bad. Let me remind you of the story of the European Payments Union. At the beginning it was very bad, because it was based almost entirely on credit, that is, on the purely arbitrary creation of means of foreign payment. At the end, it was nearly entirely good—I mean efficient—because it was made increasingly "harder" as a result of the increase in the proportion of settlements effected in gold.

F.H. M. Rueff, in 1958 you presided over a committee which laid the basis for French financial recovery, by what was called then *assainissement*. It included, besides many disinflationary measures, devaluation and an exposure of the economy to competition. Now, some people in Britain think that we might be able to do with some *assainissement* ourselves just now. If Mr. Wilson were to appoint you to head a similar committee for our problems, what recommendations might a Rueff report for Britain make?

J.R. May I first state emphatically that I am not a candidate for

[9] The day General de Gaulle held his press conference dealing with the gold problem.

such an assignment. And secondly, that I would first ask to be informed on the situation, which I am not today. I can only say that from the outside I do not have the feeling—it is only an impression—that there is a great financial problem in the United Kingdom. I always live under the impression that Britain is the country that has the highest financial tradition and the best equipment in the field of credit. The London market is a model, and for twenty-five years I have been fighting for the introduction of its practice in France. Though I must say that M. Giscard d'Estaing has made progress in this field. He has taken steps that are certainly in the right direction, but there remains much to be done. You do have the problem of the sterling balances held by foreigners, and that is a difficult one.

F.H. May I just ask you a question in connection with successful domestic policies? France's two great periods of economic success in the last generation were after the stabilization cum devaluation of the franc in 1926–1928 and after 1958. Both of these stabilizations were at a decidedly undervalued exchange rate, and I believe you had some personal influence both times. Do you believe that, in any program for Britain, this might have any lessons for us?

J.R. There is one point I must make clear for the sake of history. I was associated with the Poincaré stabilization only to a very small degree. I was a young *inspecteur des finances* and I was called as one of his assistant secretaries to study only one question—which was the exchange rate.

F.H. The most important question.

J.R. I said—and it has now been published[10]—that the key consideration was to find the level at which you would not have to reduce money wages. Contrast your experience in 1925.

[10] The report, addressed in 1926 to the Prime Minister who was also Finance Minister, was published under the title *"Sur un point d'histoire: le niveau de la stabilisation Poincaré,"* Revue politique, 1969 (Editions du Recueil, Surey). The text has been reproduced in full in *Les Fondements philosophiques des système économiques* (Payol, 1967), p. 415.

The main principle is that you must create a situation in which in no case do you have to get a reduction in domestic money wages. However, if you stabilize at a price level which as regards gold and foreign currencies is slightly lower than the floor price, you have a safety margin which may provide substantial advantages. But it would be a great mistake to have this margin without using it to do very quickly what remains to be done.

In 1958—and there I know the situation full well—the principal merit of the plan was that it was global, comprehensive. That does not mean I was satisfied with what was done later, because what was lacking in the development of this policy was a decided improvement of our credit system, which is still obsolete, and the diminution of the rigidities in the French economy. And I think if I had any responsibility in London, I would make a thorough investigation of the source of rigidities in the British economy, that means all the matters dealt with in my second report (1959–1960) on the "obstacles to economic expansion." I was considering in particular the problems of distribution, the structure of the various markets, rents, farm prices, and all the protected sectors of the economy. It is incredible to see what rigidities history has left in old countries like yours and mine. And yet, if you want your program of reforms to be efficacious, you must resolve all these problems simultaneously.

But let me conclude. All that has been said about the price of gold in the United States and all that has been said in every country about what is called devaluation, I have heard so many times. We in France have had great experience in this field. A devaluation or change in the price of gold is always opposed by the great majority of people. They say it is morally impossible, it is practically impossible, it would be inefficient. And I have seen it in France five or six times in my own career, and several times also in Britain. Now we see that, once done, it was easily accepted, and that in every case it was, at least in the short run, successful—provided it

was part of a general policy of economic and financial restoration. The only trouble is that we have not always used the
resulting period of rest to do what we meant to do.

In your case I have no specific advice to offer. The consideration of the world monetary problem that is bound to be
undertaken in the near future may provide an occasion to
look at the special problem of sterling and maybe also of
the sterling area.

# VI

## TIME FOR ACTION

General de Gaulle's statement, my own interview with *The Economist*, and several lectures I delivered in France and abroad, together with the deterioration of the U.S. monetary situation as a result of gold losses and the increasing accumulation of dollar balances, had drawn attention to the problem of the international monetary system, but had had no impact on the position of the U.S. authorities or the intergovernmental committees that they influence (the Committee of Ten, Working Party No. 3 of the OEEC, the Board of Governors of the IMF). The following chapters tell the long and sorry tale of the monetary situation over the years 1965 and 1966.

For my part, I was ever more convinced as time went by that the progressive deterioration of the situation would inevitably lead to a serious monetary mishap, likely to have disastrous consequences and inflict profound sufferings upon large groups of the population. I felt that the time was past for allusive statements that remained obscure to the large part of public opinion that was not sufficiently conversant with the problem to grasp all the subtle implications and euphemisms. I felt it my duty to make clear that my position was not merely one of criticism, but was directed toward constructive action. I therefore resolved to set out in full daylight the components of an effective and lasting solution.

It goes without saying that my proposed arrangements were not the only feasible ones and that other solutions were conceivable, for instance, solutions based on the consolidation on an amicable basis of part of the dollar or sterling balances.

My program was set out in an article published in France in *Le Monde* of 27 September 1966, and in Britain in *The Times (Business Review)* of 26 September, under the title "Allegiance to Outdated Fetish."

*Le Monde* introduced my article with the following remark:

> For Mr. Jacques Rueff, the time for patching up the existing system is long past. Mr. Rueff vindicates his contentions with increased vigor, advocating a revaluation of gold, which in his view would bring about "a lasting wave of prosperity."

There followed, under the title which heads this chapter, the text of the article:

Five years have passed since I raised in these columns the problem of the international monetary system.

During these sixty months there have been many discussions between experts and two reports setting out their differences.[1] But there has been no action. Or rather, the actions that have been accomplished—the Roosa bonds, swaps, general loan agreements, and increases in the International Monetary Fund quotas—were merely aimed at prolonging an international system that in any case could not last.

While governments were deliberating but not acting, the process that I had predicted and described in my articles published in 1961 continued to unfold inexorably, with all attendant effects: the con-

[1] The Ossola Report in 1965 and the reports of alternates to the Ministers and Governors of the Group of Ten in July 1966.

tinuing U.S. balance-of-payments deficit, notwithstanding ever-renewed statements by the American authorities announcing that the deficit had been brought under control and was going to be finally eliminated; inflationary trends in countries with balance-of-payments surpluses; the progressive deterioration of the solvency of the key-currency countries as a result of a steady increase in dollar and sterling balances, and a concomitant dwindling of their gold stocks.

Today no one doubts that the decline has entered its final phase: that of collapse, by resorption of the monetary assets that the dollar balances constitute and, to a certain extent as well—although the problem they present is different—the sterling balances.

I would not agree that these threats are the sole result of the conversion into gold of dollar balances belonging to France. In 1965, payments of gold to France represented little more than 50 percent of the total gold outflow from the United States. Besides, could it be imagined that creditors, who are not blinded or tied by political dependence, would wait undismayed until the assets that are the counterpart of their claim have vanished?

The consequences of the collapse, if we allow it to happen, would be tragic. We can foresee them with certainty, if we observe the familarity that exists, *mutatis mutandis,* between what is happening now and what happened in the years 1928–1933.

Let us not forget, as regards the latter, the sterling crisis, the attempts made to find a solution through internal deflation, the political difficulties which led to the formation of a national coalition government under Ramsay Macdonald, the whole culminating in the devaluation of the pound in 1931.

Let us not forget either the tremendous disaster of the Great Depression, carrying in its wake countless sufferings and widespread ruin, a catastrophe that was brought under control only in 1934, when President Roosevelt, after a complex mix of remedies had proved unavailing, raised the price of gold from $20 to $35 an ounce.

At that time, France, which had just completed its financial rehabilitation operation of 1928, was the last but not the least to be adversely affected. It is no mere chance that the magnitude of the rehabilitation operation carried out in 1958 provides a temporary shelter from the storm, as was the case thirty-five years ago.

Even the absurd discussions on the inadequacy of existing liquidity had their counterpart in 1928 and 1929 in the preposterous debates of the Gold Committee of the League of Nations.

Are we passively to watch the onslaught of catastrophes similar to those of the depression?

I am sure they could still be avoided, provided it is accepted that we act swiftly.

## THE NECESSARY STEPS

So that I do not repeat the mistake of the doctors who were discussing the sex of the angels when the enemy, Crisis, was already within the walls, I shall confine myself to enumerating the actions that are vital. I have so often demonstrated the necessity of such action that I invite the reader wishing to receive explanations or justifications to refer to my previous publications.

Effecting a solution implies an agreement between all countries with convertible currency (the Group of Ten plus a few others) by which they would undertake:

1. Not to increase appreciably from a given date their monetary assets in dollars and sterling. This undertaking would not be an obstacle to the acquisition of dollars and sterling for the purpose of settlement within reasonable limits.

2. To increase simultaneously the price at which their banks of issue buy and sell gold in their respective markets. The amount of this increase would be established by common agreement. But one can foresee that it will bring on an approximate doubling in the price of gold, if gold is to be restored to its rightful place in the price hierarchy, account being taken of the changes which occurred in the cost of production of the yellow metal.

3. The United States and Britain would undertake to use all the increase in nominal value of their respective gold stocks for im-

mediate repayment, in gold, of the dollar and sterling balances held by the banks of issue or the public authorities of other countries.

Implementation of this undertaking would in effect wipe out the dollar balance, but would only reduce by about one-sixth existing sterling balances.

4. Countries holding gold but with no balances to repay, in effect all countries with convertible currency other than Britain and the United States, would agree to offer Britain, in the form of a twenty-year loan, the fraction of the nominal value increment of their gold stock necessary for the repayment in gold of the residual sterling balances that had not already been consolidated and which the British Government considered needed to be repaid. The latter alone, in fact, could determine their amount, for the sterling balances—which to a large extent belong to international organizations or Commonwealth countries—are much less volatile than the dollar balances.

At all events, such use, if it is desired by the British Government—and it is neither certain nor perhaps essential that it would be—would absorb only a relatively small part of the value increment that the rise in the price of gold would generate for countries having reserves of the metal and no balances to repay.

5. The same countries would allocate another part (to be determined) of the nominal value increment of their gold stocks (left over after the preceding operation) for aid to developing countries.

How this is to be used would be decided by common agreement. This could be either in the form of a direct loan, the creation of capital through an international organization with power to borrow in the market, or through an increase in the capital of one of the existing agencies.

6. Finally, the same countries would undertake to use, as fully as possible, that part of the nominal value increment which they will retain after methods 3, 4, and 5 have been resorted to, for repayment of their debts, especially for the repayment in gold of their debts to their respective banks of issue.

## LASTING WAVE OF PROSPERITY

If such pledges are fulfilled, they will save the world from the threat that the rapid extension of exchange controls in the United States brings to bear on international relations, in particular on such trade as has already been freed. The possibility of an embargo on U.S. gold would cease to block the economic horizon of the West.

Britain would no longer have to impose upon itself the impossible task of effecting a drastic deflation to repay, out of the surpluses of its balance of payments, which at present runs a substantial deficit, the sterling balances that are the outcome of its past administration and, in particular, of its war effort. Being freed from this worry, Britain could safely introduce the internal reforms which seem necessary to it.

As for the developing countries, they would find in the above-mentioned plan tangible proof of the effective friendship of nations that preceded them on the road to economic maturity, and also good grounds for lasting cooperation toward the sound administration of the world's resources.

I solemnly proclaim that as soon as the event is behind us and no longer silhouetted against the horizon of all our economic prospects, the world will be carried on the crest of a lasting wave of unprecedented prosperity. With its magnitude and strength, it would provide a solution to all our problems, those of labor and those of capital, those of a welfare state like Britain and those of a free-enterprise country like the United States. A huge amount of capital that is now hoarded would flow into the markets. Long-term interest rates would fall, the means of providing hospitals, schools, roads, and houses would become available—in short, all the possibilities of noninflationary investment that determine social progress would be tremendously increased over a long period. The liberalization of international economic relations would not only be desired, but accepted by all joyfully, as was the case in France after the 1958 reform.

All this is simple and certain, and could be achieved tomorrow if the nations of the West agreed. But would they want it?

In the present state of affairs it is highly improbable that they do in fact want it. The principal if not the only obstacle results from the opposition of American public opinion to an increase in the price of gold.

It is the awareness of this opposition that accounts for the reticence of experts. As soon as it disappears, their objections will melt like snow in the sun, and they will find numerous reasons for recommending what now they are advising against.

The only problem for the West is to convince public opinion in the United States and, first and foremost, the American Government.

Admittedly, logical reasons do not always convince, but without them one has no chance of convincing anybody.

No one has even tried to talk reason to the United States. Moreover, the governments, guided by deliberate obscurantism, have forbidden the experts of the Group of Ten to place the question of the gold price on their agenda, if only to talk about it.


## HOW TO EXORCISE THE PROBLEM OF GOLD

The first task is to exorcise the problem of gold from all the prejudices and spurious arguments that encumber it.

I am convinced that as soon as the problem is considered in the light of day, the United States will be unable to say that it is a rise in the price of gold that would be unusual, but, on the contrary, its being maintained at its present level, whereas prices have more than doubled in the United States since the time it was last fixed.

To appreciate this policy one should try to imagine the sort of impact it would have if it were applied to corn or coal.

Is it reasonable to organize systematically a scarcity of gold—when the needs are almost proportional to the general level of prices—while maintaining the nominal value of existing stocks and the value of annual production at a level less than half of what it would be if the price of gold was restored to its rightful place among general market prices?

Is it reasonable and fair to give every producer of a ton of coal or steel, a weight of gold double what he would have received in exchange for his output in 1934?

Is it reasonable and fair for the United States to persist in giving the holders of dollar balances, in exchange for their holdings, a weight of gold double what they would be entitled to if, as a result of a provision that no economic consideration can justify, the price of gold, alone among all the world prices, had not been maintained at its 1934 level?

Can we validly contend that those who advocate a rise in the price of gold are damaging the legitimate interests of the United States and Britain, when, if they had been heeded five years ago, the United States and Britain would still hold half the gold that they have lost since and their creditors would legitimately see their claims to payments in gold reduced in weight by 50 percent?

It is not relevant to bring in at this point the concept of implicit moral obligations. A debtor's duty is first of all to maintain himself in a condition in which he is able to repay his debts and not to assent passively to an arrangement that will lead him inescapably to insolvency.

Last but not least, is it possible that the government and opinion of a great country, mindful more than any other of its responsibilities, which with incomparable courage has assumed the duties devolving upon it by reason of its power and wealth, should persist in exposing the people of the world to the throes of another depression, simply because it wishes to maintain, in a mood of childish frowardness, the outdated fetish of a gold price fixed arbitrarily in 1934, when conditions were entirely different from those which exist at this time?

In our age of conscious action, of operational research, of reasoned policy, will the world be foolish enough obstinately to refuse its salvation?

But it is late—later than you think. Action is urgently needed. Will it come in time?

# VII

---

## TRIFFIN AND I

For a long time public opinion tended to look on the monetary controversy as a duel between Robert Triffin, the well-known American professor at Yale University, and myself.

Both he and I have always protested against this oversimplified representation of our views which, although they differed in their conclusions, stemmed from a common diagnosis and were based on the same reasoning.

Early in July 1966 Mr. Michel Gabrysiak, an eminent journalist, arranged a face-to-face session between the two of us and gave the following account of our discussion, which was published in *l'Aurore* of 4 July and the Sunday *Times* of 3 July 1966:

RUEFF. Unless the international monetary system is reformed quickly and efficiently, the world is threatened with serious disorder, not only in the monetary field but also—and this is more serious—in the economic and social sectors. The memory of what happened in 1931 causes considerable concern in this respect.

TRIFFIN. I fully agree. The most serious trouble spots at present are the recurrent crises of sterling and the dollar. A few years ago, an attack on one of these currencies helped the other because capital shifts were from London to New York or vice versa. To-day, a grave crisis in sterling automatically engenders a crisis for the dollar, and for other world currencies as well.

## THE FUNDAMENTAL WEAKNESS OF THE SYSTEM

RUEFF. This situation is the result of the use, over an extended period, of a well-known system, the gold-exchange standard. The result of the operation of this system is that, when the United States, for example, has a deficit, it pays dollars that are returned the same day to New York, where they are reinvested.

The deficit therefore does not affect the abundant supply of funds in New York; in this way, the deficits can continue indefinitely.

TRIFFIN. I agree entirely. Mr. Rueff has expressed, in a way to which I subscribe 99 percent, our two essential points of agreement. It is unsound to allow a country to secure automatic financing of its deficits.

## NEGOTIATING ON A VOLCANO

Even if America regains its balance, the sudden liquidation of past debts could trigger serious disturbances.

Mr. Rueff was saying: this can happen any day. In fact, it happened last year. In 1965, the European countries, which until then had accumulated $1 billion to $2 billion per year, liquidated inside twelve months more than $2 billions of reserve currency and converted it to gold.

We continue not exactly dancing on a volcano but in fact negotiating at a snail's pace on a volcano which may erupt all of a sudden—which, in fact, did erupt right under our feet in September 1931. I am prepared to admit that cooperation between central banks has since then been expanded. But all the palliatives that have been adopted since then have simply helped us carry on—dangerously. If this had not been the case, the crisis of September 1931 would have been repeated already in October

1960. To a great extent, all this is due to the monetary and financial situation of my country, the United States. From 1951 to 1955, we received $500 million of short-term capital each year. In the second half of the fifties, we received, on the average, $1 billion a year.

In 1960, we lost about $2.3 billion as a result of a sudden reversal of the trend.

Starting from 1960 to the end of 1964 we lost an average of $1.5 billion a year of short-term capital. In the aggregate, this represents an average turnaround, over a period of ten years, of $2.5 billion a year. This amount is roughly equal to the total U.S. balance-of-payments deficits over the last five or six years.

What was the situation last year? Self-imposed restrictions reduced the outflow of capital from the United States. But these measures affected only U.S. residents, whereas, to finance their investments, corporations borrow in the European market the capital that they need, which means probably $1 billion in 1966. To face these new demands, Europeans need to repatriate some of the capital they keep in the United States.

As a result, we lose on the one side what we gain on the other. Export of capital continues, especially since foreign assets in the United States amount to some $57 billion.

The extension of military operations in Vietnam has also contributed to the deterioration of our balance of payments, not only on external account but from the point of view of internal repercussions. The economic boom that accompanies the war in Vietnam has led to inflationary pressures, which in turn have adversely affected the balance of payments to the extent of $2 billion.

In 1966, the U.S. deficit will, I am afraid, be closer to $3 billion rather than $2 billion.


## ANY INCIDENT CAN TRIGGER OFF A CRISIS

RUEFF. We can see that the brakes are already operating and that everything we observe—the shrinking of financial availabilities, the slowdown of expansion, the mitigation of the overheating of the economy—is not attributable to chance but to the process that Mr. Triffin and I had long foreseen. This shows that our fears were not unjustified.

Until now this has been a quiet and slow-moving process, but any event can trigger off an avalanche and the situation is very touch-and-go.

A sudden deterioration would spell the disappearance of all the progress achieved over the past ten years in the fields of trade liberalization and the improvement of the standard of living.

Can one seriously allow the immense weight of the international monetary system to rest on the currency of two countries with constant balance-of-payments deficits? This situation is truly preposterous, and what is worse, it can only disappear through the elimination of the gold-exchange standard that produced it.

TRIFFIN. The situation is all the more serious since the only operational agreement reached by the Group of Ten is that any reform of the international system must depend on the U.S. balance-of-payments equilibrium. Yet the U.S. balance-of-payments is—at least to a large extent—the outcome of the present system.

## A SIN AGAINST HUMAN INTELLIGENCE

RUEFF. This is a basic point of agreement between Mr. Triffin and me. It is really a sin against human intelligence to claim that a reform is not feasible so long as the U.S. balance-of-payments deficit continues.

TRIFFIN. It cannot disappear since it is the outcome of the system.

RUEFF. There is therefore a fundamental mistake that I have consistently denounced and to which we must call the attention of the general public. To wait for the deficit to disappear before introducing a reform is to remain in a vicious circle which we must break one day and from which, alas, events will eventually free us if we are not wise enough to free ourselves voluntarily.

I further believe that there is no need to increase the volume of international liquidity.

There are, however, two countries that lack the means to keep paying for their deficit without losing gold: they are the United States and Britain. What they need is not international liquidities *in abstracto* but francs, marks, lire, etc., etc.

## A FAULT THAT CANNOT BE ATONED FOR

For the time being the real problem is concealed from our sight, and this is very serious, because it has allowed the United States and Britain to settle their deficits without losing gold. I consider this a mistake that cannot be atoned for, because it has masked the true nature of the problem.

TRIFFIN. One of the solutions that looks essential to me is the consolidation of the commitments inherited from the past, because the first problem to resolve is to avoid a world monetary crisis that would be provoked by massive gold withdrawals. Economists belong to different schools, but we all agree on the need to eliminate the gold-exchange standard promptly.

RUEFF. The plan that I have prepared to that end is intended to restore the efficiency of the international payments mechanism. But, mind, the question now is not a return to the gold standard. We already have it. The proof of it is that those countries that want to get some gold from the United States can easily get it.

The problem is not one of introducing in any way a new system but only to cure the existing one of a small cancer that has affected its functioning. Cancer is not always visible but is frequently a cause of death.

## A PREPOSTEROUS CONTENTION IS ASCRIBED TO ME

I should also wish to emphasize another aspect of the problem. People keep saying that I want to return to gold and gold alone. That is preposterous! The question is not in any way to eliminate the existing credit superstructure, with all its flexibility and all its adjustment capabilities. These constitute one of the essential aspects of the true gold standard.

The most rational solution, it seems to me, is to observe that, although the price of gold was fixed in 1934 at $35 an ounce by President Roosevelt, all prices in the United States have doubled, leaving gold far behind.

If we accept the hypothesis of a doubling of the price of gold— and I am not against a smaller increase—the gold stock of the United States, now $13.5 billion, would be worth $27 billion.

The United States could use the increment to reimburse the claims in the hands of the foreign banks of issue, which amount to $15 to $16 billion. The nominal value of the quantity of gold which would then be left in Fort Knox would still approximate the nominal value of the present gold stock, but the U.S. debts resulting from the dollar balances would have been settled.

Obviously, such an operation could only take place through the signing of an international agreement providing for a simultaneous increase in the price of gold in all convertible-currency countries.

My solution would be highly beneficial to the United States, whereas the view is generally held that it would affect it adversely.

## MR. AMERICA GETS THE POINT

Let me tell you what happened to me during my last visit to the United States. I met an extremely important Senator. He received me very roughly and declared: "I understand the purpose of your policy. You want to take all our gold, double the price, and so make an enormous profit at our expense." I replied: "Mr. Senator, it's exactly the reverse. I advise you to double the price of gold so long as you have some left, and to give us only half the weight that you persist in giving us now in exchange for our dollars at the prevailing rate of conversion." Whereupon he threw up his arms and ejaculated: "Why, if that is what you propose, I could not agree more!" "That is indeed the meaning of my proposal," I concluded.

# REVALUATION OF GOLD:
## A TIDAL WAVE OF INFLATION

TRIFFIN. I, too, condemn the gold-exchange standard as it exists now. But I do not think that one could improve the system by going back to the pure gold standard, that is, by eliminating the exchange component.

The supply of monetary gold throughout the world depends on a country threatened by civil war, namely, the Union of South Africa, and on the USSR, which provides on the average two-thirds of the new gold reserves that accrue to central banks each year. Disappearance due to speculation and private hoarding exceeds Western production of gold.

A revaluation of gold would be followed by a tidal wave of inflation that would spread all over the world. I therefore do not agree with Mr. Rueff on this point. I believe that before there is any reevaluation of gold we must come to a world agreement on the elimination of the exchange component from the international reserve system, with the exception of the necessary cash holdings.

Then, of course, the past must be fully written off.

If we cannot reach agreement, the reevaluation of gold will come as the result of a catastrophe.

There will be an unplanned devaluation, which could be a tragic repetition of the thirties.

## LET'S HELP BRITAIN FIRST

RUEFF. I am glad to hear Mr. Triffin say so. I see that we are in full agreement as regards the diagnosis. I agree with Mr. Triffin when he says that doubling or increasing the price of gold could create a danger of inflation. This is why I urge that, at the same time, both dollar and sterling balances be repaid.

Futhermore, since we know that Great Britain is in a difficult position, I propose that surplus countries extend a twenty-year loan to Great Britain for the reimbursement of outstanding un consolidated sterling balances.

TRIFFIN. I suggest an immediate agreement between the eight richest countries in the world, that is, the United States, Great Britain, Switzerland, Belgium-Luxembourg, France, Germany, Italy, and the Netherlands. The exchange component of the reserves of the central banks of these countries would not exceed 15 percent of the total. The rest should be in gold.

They would set up an international organization whose function it would be to convert into gold any amount of the exchange component in excess of the 15 percent ratio. Only Germany and Italy run such surpluses. The operation would cost $1.5 billion worth of gold. All other outstanding debts would be consolidated. A gold guarantee would be attached to the currency amounts held by the organization. The consequence would be that the dollar and sterling components of the central bank reserves would disappear altogether, leaving only the remaining 15 percent to serve as the necessary cash reserve.

RUEFF. This is a very logical and sound project. Nevertheless, I believe it has no chance whatsoever of being accepted in this form, mainly on account of the discrimination it establishes between the eight countries and other countries also in a creditor position vis-à-vis the United States.

As for the gold guarantee for dollars and sterling, I think it would be a dangerous thing, because the result would be that this clause would make it difficult, if not impossible, to write off the past.

TRIFFIN. I know that these problems exist. In fact, the other countries that are in a creditor position vis-à-vis the United States will not try to convert into gold because it is a tradition with them to hold dollars.

# PART THREE

# Enter the Experts

# VIII

---

## THE GENERAL CLIMATE

The views recorded in the previous chapters—those expressed by General de Gaulle in his message of 4 February 1965 and those that I myself had set forth in my three articles of June 1961, in the interview with *The Economist* of 13 February 1965, and in the program of action published by *Le Monde* on 27 September 1966—were violently assailed.

There were very few who thought that the remarks made by the President of the Republic reflected a well-thought-out opinion as to the nature of the mechanisms likely to ensure internal stability and international order. Most commentators viewed them as the expression of an underlying anti-American feeling aimed at causing, for political purposes, an increasing deterioration of American solvency through the exchange against gold of the dollar balances held by creditor countries. Such was in particular the reaction of U.S. public opinion, which was especially vehement.

It never occurred to these critics that only gold transfers could operate to restore the equilibrium of the U.S. external payments, through the variations in global demand which, *ceteris paribus,* would inevitably result. They would not admit that the net result would be that the return-to-gold policy would be more in the interest of the United States than of the creditor countries, because the latter, by requesting reimbursement of their dollars, would in fact be only exercising a right that had been formally conferred upon them and confirmed on many occasions. These critics never mentioned the fact that the United States, for its part, was holding only insignificant amounts of foreign currencies in its monetary reserves, and that what it regarded as essential could also be a good thing as far as other convertible-currency countries were concerned.

As to my own statements, they gave rise in French official circles to many reservations and much criticism. I have already reported the opinion expressed by the Finance Minister in his letter of 8 December 1961 (see page 68). His views were shared by many young technocrats and several of the professors under whom they had studied. As far as they were concerned, the view that there could be no influence likely to coordinate the sum total of individual behavior by means of incentives was an article of faith based on deep-rooted political conviction. They were of the opinion that international trade is the outcome of structural situations and administrative interventions designed to correct them. These neophytes, who refused to acknowledge the virtue of all economic mechanisms, considered that the dollar gap which existed in Europe prior to 1958 was a structural phenomenon that neither monetary and fiscal policy nor interest rates could in any way affect. And it was also they who, after the last world war, advocated pegged discount rates and had them maintained in force for a long period, whereas more recent history has shown *a contrario* how unavailing and harmful such rates were.

The shift from a dollar scarcity to a dollar glut situation, when in 1958 most European currencies became convertible again, did not shake the stubborn conviction of these superficial glossarists. They persist in seeing in the mentions that are made in support of cybernetic regulating influences—which are nothing more than the ordinary stuff that all natural phenomena are made of—an outmoded conjuring up of the "invisible hand" of Adam Smith, and forget that the idol they revere without understanding him (I mean

Lord Keynes) stated in an article published by the *Economic Journal* after his death, in June 1946:

> I find myself moved, not for the first time, to remind our contemporary economists that the classical teaching embodies some permanent truths of great significance, which we are liable today to overlook because we associated them with other doctrines which we cannot now accept without much qualification. There are in these matters deep undercurrents at work, neutral forces, one can call them, or even the invisible hand,[1] which are operating towards equilibrium. If it were not so, we could not have got on even so well as we have for many decades past. . . . And if we reject the medicine from our systems altogether, we may just drift on from expedient to expedient and never really get fit again.

In the United States, public opinion as a whole was hostile to my conclusions, in particular to the extent that they referred to the price of gold. However, several high monetary authorities received with sympathetic understanding the principle of my analysis, not without denying, however, the remedy that it had led me to propose. The many invitations that I received to speak in public afforded evidence of the interest with which my contentions were received. Thus, I had occasion to expound them on 15 April 1965 in New York at a meeting of the National Industrial Conference Board, where I was greatly honored by the presence of Mr. Nixon, who was to become President of the United States. I also was called upon to present a monetary reconstruction program to the banking conference of the New England Board in Boston on 20 October 1967, and to the International Industrial Conference convened by the Research Institute of Stanford University and the National

[1] This is a reference to the "invisible hand" mentioned by Adam Smith in *The Wealth of Nations.*

Industrial Conference Board at San Francisco on 15 September 1969.

I must pay a tribute to the enlightened understanding shown by two eminent friends: William McChesney-Martin, Chairman of the Federal Reserve Board, and Robert Roosa, Undersecretary of the Treasury under Presidents Kennedy and Johnson. Although opposed to an increase in the price of gold, they have consistently shown sympathy and esteem toward my endeavors. The former even invited me, in December 1961, to make my views known at a luncheon meeting of the Open Market Committee, the holy of holies of the Federal Reserve Board.

I also owe a debt of gratitude to the *Banker,* the great London periodical, which in 1969 published a detailed analysis of my San Francisco statement. The reader may be interested by the introduction that is reproduced here, because it gives an overall view of the failures of the international monetary policy over the preceding seven years:

> Man has conquered the moon. At this moment of triumph for human reason and in particular for American science, method, and technology, we cannot but praise and admire. In the sphere of astronautics everything has been foreseen. The event came as an astonishingly precise confirmation of the calculations of the scientists, the foresight of the technicians, and the skill of the organizers.
>
> In contrast, for eight years the facts have always belied the forecasting of the highest financial authorities. Must one recall the repeated declarations that the United States would put its balance of payments into full and final equilibrium?
>
> In an article in *Foreign Affairs* of October 1963 my good friend Robert Roosa wrote: "The President's program, presented on 18 July 1963, demonstrates emphatically the determination of the United States to correct its own deficit."

In July 1965 the distinguished Secretary of the Treasury, Mr. Fowler, announced that the U.S. balance-of-payments deficit would be halved before the end of the year and completely eliminated in 1966.

On 1 January 1968, the President of the United States formulated an ambitious program at San Antonio which was supposed to restore external equilibrium.

One knows what became of all these forecasts.

In another sphere, the governments all rallied to the grandiose policy of the Kennedy Plan for reducing obstacles to international trade. Well, since then, very stringent exchange controls have been set up in England and in France. Even in the United States export of capital has been severely controlled and limited in different ways.

As to interest rates, the finance ministers of France, Germany, Italy, Britain, and the United States solemnly undertook at the Chequers Conference of January 1967 to join their efforts to bring down interest rates in their respective countries to a lower level than they would otherwise have been. Events have shown how vain this undertaking was.

It is painful and unpleasant to recall these failures, but it is necessary to do so if we are to judge objectively the policies that led to them and, above all, the remedies now envisaged to restore a situation that we can see is getting worse every day.

If Armstrong, Collins, and Aldrin instead of reaching the moon had fallen back to earth, we would conclude that there had been some error in the principles on which Apollo XI was built or in the calculations of their trajectory.

The constant refutation of the monetary forecasts by the facts obliges me to recall that their failure was not fortuitous, that it was foreseeable and had in fact been foreseen.

While the champions and the opponents of the gold standard were fighting it out—the opponents being clearly more numerous than the champions—monetary events were following their own relentless course.

The years 1958, 1959, and 1960 were characterized, as far as the United States was concerned, by massive gold outflows: $1.07 billion in 1959, $1.7 billion in 1960.

In October 1960, the gold price in London reached and even exceeded for a short while $40 per ounce, as against a parity of $35. The gold pool was hastily put in place, providing joint, co-ordinated support for the dollar: 50 percent was contributed by the United States, the balance to be allocated between the other participating countries.

Again in 1961 the pound sterling was badly jolted as a result of the revaluation of the deutschmark and the guilder.

All these disturbances gave rise to a widespread feeling that the international monetary system was not so unshakable as some of its champions claimed, thereby confirming what I had written in June 1961. The governments and the monetary authorities refused to apply the remedy that I had advocated, but, being convinced by the course of events that the gold-exchange standard had become precarious, they felt under the obligation to seek adequate solutions.

The following chapter will describe the procedures followed in the preparation of these reforms.

# IX

## SYMPTOMATIC TREATMENT

Symptomatic treament is intended merely to remedy the visible effects of an ailment without getting at the underlying causes. This was the extent of the treatment that the "experts" administered when, starting in 1960, they attempted to deal with the ailing dollar.

The events recalled above were evidence that, if the existing situation continued, it would promptly lead to the exhaustion of the gold reserves of the United States and Britain. However, the financial authorities were anxious to avoid the widespread monetary crisis that would have resulted from inconvertibility of the dollar and the pound.

They would not acknowledge that the special reserve status of these two currencies was the real cause of the balance-of-payments deficit of the United States and Britain. But by the same token, these same authorities were committing themselves to remedying the consequences, that is, to helping the countries concerned to settle their external deficits.

The first consequence of these monetary difficulties was an extension of the responsibilities of the International Monetary Fund. In addition to its regular tasks, the fund had to give assistance to the pound and the dollar, which were dangerously threatened.

On 7 October 1958, at the annual meeting of the International Monetary Fund at New Delhi, the member states decided to increase the quotas, that is, the amount of their contributions to this international organization. It soon became clear, however, that this increase was not enough to enable the fund to meet all requests for switches into hard currencies.

In August 1961, Britain, which had been going through a serious monetary crisis, obtained from the fund credit facilities totaling $2 billion. This convinced the monetary authorities and the governments that there was need for providing the fund with new financing possibilities.

In September 1961, at the annual meeting of the governors of the fund in Vienna, the late managing director, Per Jacobson, suggested that the fund be authorized to borrow from member states the amount of resources needed to support currencies under severe strain.

Negotiations continued after the annual meeting between the managing director and representatives of the ten countries that were in a position to provide the currencies needed: the United States, Canada, Great Britain, France, Germany, Italy, the Netherlands, Belgium, Japan, and Sweden. Under the Paris Agreements of 15 December 1961, known as the General Arrangements to Borrow, these states undertook to lend the fund a total amount of $6 billion, of which 50 percent was to be supplied by the United States and Britain, the balance being shared among the other eight signatories. The preamble to the agreement stipulates that each state shall make available the amount of the loan it has undertaken to provide when the ten states, in agreement with the International Monetary Fund, recognize under a voting procedure specified in the agreement that "supplementary resources are needed to forestall or cope with an impairment of the international monetary system."

This declaration of intention is significant. It shows that the signatory states, confronted with certain balance-of-payments deficits, are more anxious to provide debtor countries with the foreign exchange necessary for the settlement of their external commitments than to remedy the underlying cause of their difficulties.

Some claim that the talks that had been scheduled between the managing director of the fund and the executive directors representing the participating states could have afforded an occasion for making adequate recommendations. But the context and subsequent developments of the consultation procedure afford sufficient evidence that, in the minds of the sponsors of the agreement—as is the tradition with the International Monetary Fund—such recommendations would be addressed to the domestic situation of the deficit countries, and not to the international monetary system under which they were operating.

Nevertheless, in 1961 the persistence and magnitude of the U.S. balance-of-payments deficit induced the American Treasury to intervene in the foreign exchange market through the Bank for International Settlements. To this end, the Federal Reserve Bank of New York, together with some ten foreign central banks, entered into swap agreements. A swap is a transaction whereby two banks, and in particular two central banks, exchange equivalent amounts in their respective currencies for a certain length of time—usually three to six months—with possible extension, final unwinding being effected on the basis of the rates initially agreed upon. This arrangement amounted in fact to an exchange guarantee for the partners.

In late August 1964, the swap agreements entered into by the Federal Reserve Bank of New York constituted supplementary credit facilities amounting to about $2 billion.

Although swap agreements were in general on a renewable basis, they were nothing more than short-term facilities. The American Treasury, desirous of consolidating its debt by means of longer-term bilateral loans, issued nonnegotiable Treasury bills, which were taken up by foreign, and more specifically European, central banks. These were the Roosa bonds, named after the Undersecretary of the Treasury who initiated the scheme.

The Roosa bonds, which were generally denominated in the

currency of the lending country and therefore involved an exchange guarantee for that country, were initially issued in 1962 to take up substantial dollar holdings accumulated by the Italian Exchange Office. But they soon came to include a clause enabling the central bank of the subscribing country to exchange the bonds against American Treasury bonds, which could also be mobilized. Thus the amounts loaned by the central banks in the form of Roosa bonds continued to be included in the exchange reserves of the lending country, just like the dollar balances that were the outcome of the gold-exchange standard.

# X

## THE CRITICAL ERROR
## IN THE DIAGNOSIS:
## THE INTERNATIONAL
## LIQUIDITY SHORTAGE

The continuing nature and the scope of the U.S. balance-of-payments deficit eventually convinced the governments and the banks of issue that all the above-mentioned cash facilities were mere expedients and did not in any way resolve the problems arising out of the dollar situation.

On 2 October 1963 the ministers and governors of the member countries of the Group of Ten, meeting in Washington on the occasion of the annual session·of the International Monetary Fund, decided at last to deal with the substance of the problem.

The communiqué issued at the end of the meeting contains the following passage:

> The ministers and governors have thought it useful that an exhaustive study be undertaken of the prospects regarding the functioning of the international monetary system and probable future liquidity requirements. This study should be more specifically addressed to the possible magnitude and nature of the future reserve require-

ments and supplementary credit facilities which might arise. . . . The ministers and the governors have re-affirmed their belief that a structure based, like the present structure, on fixed rates of exchange and a stable price for gold has demonstrated its value as a base on which the future can be built. . . .

The smooth operation of the international monetary system implies that there should be no major lasting international disequilibria, and that if any were to occur the governments would effectively resort to appropriate policies. That is why the ministers and the governors have decided that an exhaustive study should be made of the measures and instruments that would be most likely to lead to attainment of this objective. . . .

It will be noted, in connection with this communiqué, that a procedure which provides for and directs the "exhaustive study" of the problem to be carried out, but anticipates the conclusions before the study has been undertaken, is indeed a very odd one. It states, although to my knowledge no examination of the matter had even been started, that "a structure based on fixed rates of exchange and a stable price for gold has demonstrated its value as a base on which the future can be built." This statement precluded the high authorities entrusted with the study from investigating a whole segment of the field that they were instructed to explore.

However that may be, the Washington communiqué outlines the program of work for the experts. Between September 1963 and September 1966, the work included an exploratory stage, followed by a period of decisions that were to modify profoundly the structure of the international monetary system.

The exploratory stage can be broken down into three different periods: the period of the Group of Ten, under Roosa's chairmanship; the period of the Ossola Group; and the period of the Emminger report.

The Roosa Group studied mainly three different plans:

—The Bernstein Plan, which proposed a reserve unit, to be issued by a central agency as against deposits in national currencies with that agency

—The Triffin Plan, under which the IMF would have become a bank of issue for the creation of international liquidity

—The Maudling Plan, which proposed an ingenious device under which the IMF or some other agency willing to do so would take over all sterling balances

The Ossola Group first envisaged the creation of a "collective reserve unit," an idea of Bernstein's that had been sponsored by the French experts.

After the de Gaulle press conference dealing with the problem of gold, however, France abandoned this scheme, which was immediately taken over by Mr. Fowler, then U.S. Secretary of the Treasury. He then brought up to date a statement (which I have already quoted) that had been made to me by a high American monetary official in respect to the years 1962 and 1963. Fowler presented a program for the rehabilitation of the U.S. balance of payments and stated that the deficit would be reduced by half by the end of 1965 and fully eliminated in the following year. The Treasury Secretary concluded that it was therefore essential to prepare for "the deliberate creation of a reserve instrument that would make it possible to increase international liquidity so as to meet trade requirements, in the absence of any steady increase in dollar holdings which was no longer to be expected."[1]

When I took cognizance of this suggestion, I thought it necessary to denounce the fraud that consisted of calling "creation of international liquidity" a project whose sole purpose was to furnish to the United States, and to some extent to Britain, non-American and non-British currencies as required by their respective balance-of-payments deficits. I uttered a word of caution on

[1] This analysis is largely taken from an article published in the French periodical *Banque* in November 1968.

the eve of a conference that I knew was irrevocably to commit the West to a liquidity-increase policy. My hope was not that I could impede the project, but that I could at least induce serious reflection as to the dangerous consequences involved on the part of those who would be called upon to examine it.

My article to that effect, which was published in *Le Monde* of 24 September 1966 and in *The Times* of the same date, is fully reproduced in the following chapter.

# XI

## IRRIGATION PLANS
## DURING THE FLOOD

The problem of international liquidity is at the forefront of the political news. The governments of the Group of Ten have even instructed the Ossola Committee, so named after its chairman, to draw up a report for them on the "creation of instruments of reserve," that is to say, of supplementary means for international settlements.

This is quite a remarkable document. Its authors have carried out their instructions with a rigor and an objectivity that are beyond praise. May I be permitted, however, to consider their work with the candor of the child in the tale by Hans Andersen, who dared to say that the Emperor, whose sumptuous clothes the courtiers were enthusiastically admiring, was naked.

The study of the problem of international liquidity, as dealt with in the Ossola Report, is a fascinating academic exercise, but bears no relation to the problems of the present time or with those that will arise in the near future.

The "stabilization plans" and the "income policies" that are rife in most Western countries prove overabundantly that there is currently not a shortage but an excess of monetary liquidity. The problem for these countries, where inflation remains a threat, is not to create but to neutralize the overflow of money that the U.S. balance-of-payments deficit has generously spread over the world.

This opinion is also held by the Chairman of the Federal Reserve Board, Mr. McChesney Martin. On August 30, before a Senate subcommittee, he declared that in his view "the current problem was the consequence not of a shortage but of an excess of liquidity." He did not exclude the possibility, however, that there might be "a longer term problem in this field."

In the same session, another speaker pointed out that according to the recent declarations of Herr Schmücker, West German Minister for Economic Affairs, "the German Federal Government saw no need for additional liquidity in the foreseeable future."

Finally, for Mr. Alfred Hayes, President of the Federal Reserve Bank of New York, " the whole of European thinking on the question of international liquidity comes down to this: is there a means of forcing the United States to put an end to the big balance-of-payments deficits, which create on the European Continent embarrassing excesses of liquidities and, without meaning to, cause them to increase regularly."[1]

In other words, it is only when the flood has ended that the problem studied by the governments will possibly arise. Is it wise, while the rain is still falling, to occupy so many eminent experts with the search for means of combating a possible drought and to distract their attention from the vital and urgent struggle against the flood?

On the other hand, if there is no shortage of liquidity in the world, the United States and Britain, the poles of the two zones of the gold-exchange standard, are cruelly short of the means of international payments. By this I mean nondollar and nonsterling currencies that would be necessary for them if they were to cover the deficits of their respective balances of payments without a new loss of gold and without recourse to new loans from their creditors.

It is an unacceptable euphemism and a scandalous show of

[1] Hearing before the Subcommittee on National Security and International Operations, U.S. Senate, p. 212–213.

hypocrisy to describe as the creation of "international liquidity" the many operations, such as swaps, issuing of Roosa bonds, general agreements to borrow, and increasing the quotas of the International Monetary Fund, by means of which external payments have been supplied to the United States over the past few years and, more recently, to Britain. Their purpose was in no way to resolve a shortage of liquidity that would have been a problem of general concern, but only to alleviate the difficulties caused for both countries by the demands for money with which they were confronted.

The disadvantage of this misnomer is apparent when one observes that on August 31 a leading U.S. financial paper recorded the opinion of one of its correspondents, according to whom "new instruments of reserve should be created in order that it should no longer be necessary for the United States to maintain a deficit in its balance of payments for the sole purpose of providing adequate reserves for the rest of the world."

This statement reminded me of the remark of a Minister of Finance, short of money, who said he floated loans not to fill his hard-pressed Treasury but simply to give his political friends an opportunity to record their confidence in his management. It is a misrepresentation of the same type to say that the shortage of means available to the United States and Britain for the settlement of their external deficit is the result of a general shortage of liquidity.

It should not be said that the developing countries are in the same position. Certainly they, too, lack foreign resources, but the resources they need can only be provided by loan operations, and not by the hoax of a monetary creation dressed up as an operation in the general interest.

The difficulties of the United States and Britain are likely to intensify if, as a result of a financial incident somewhere in the world, the holders of dollar or sterling balances increase their demands for repayment. In any case, the problem will present itself in all its acuteness the day that these two countries decide, in order to regain their financial independence, to settle of their own free will the dangerous liabilities represented by their monetary "balances."

If they do this—and they will do it eventually—they will free the world from the dangers that these volatile deficits present to the stability and prosperity of the Western world.

On that day an operation of international solidarity will be essential and legitimate. But it will not consist of the creation of supplementary instruments of reserve required by a world shortage of international liquidity. It will consist of a liquidation operation, in which debtors and creditors will be equally concerned, bearing the responsibility for it in common because of the spirit of compliance and the wantonness with which they have jointly accepted the monetary practices that have given rise to the present difficulties.

In disguising under the mask of the general interest the creation of resources that are required solely in view of U.S. and British indebtedness, the governments of the rest of the Group of Ten have made a mistake that has led to serious technical consequences. It has led them to accept the creation of supplementary liquidity without tying its use explicitly to the settlement of existing balances. They dealt a deadly blow to the stability and prosperity of the West when they did not make such a settlement the condition of the operations generating additional means of payment.

Let no one see in the above remarks a stance hostile to the United States or Britain. There is one thing in particular that you must not withhold from your friends, and that is the truth, above all when their fate is at stake. My intention as I tell them the truth is to dissuade them from the misleading appearances of a deceitful diagnosis and the phantasmagoria of delusive remedies.

Acknowledging the plain, unvarnished truth is the first prerequisite of an efficacious reform of the international monetary system. Such a reform will provide the necessary basis for continuing economic development and social progress. Let us hope it will not come too late.

# XII

## IMPLEMENTING THE
## WASHINGTON DIRECTIVES

The task of implementing the decisions made in Washington on 28 September 1965, during the International Monetary Fund meeting, was entrusted to a committee under the chairmanship of Dr. Emminger, Vice President of the Bundesbank.

These decisions are incorporated in a communiqué which proclaims, in the first place, the determination of the reserve currency countries (the United States and, in an ancillary way, Britain) to restore their balance-of-payments equilibrium without further delay.

The futility of such statements with regard to subsequent dollar-balance developments should make even the blind see. It shows decisively the superb indifference of balances of payments to governmental exhortations when these are made within the context of an international monetary system which, in the case of reserve currency countries, produces nothing but external deficits.

The communiqué further calls upon the OECD to set up a system of strict "multilateral surveillance" and entrusts it with the task of keeping under review the modalities of the settlement of existing deficits.

This task of surveillance, which took the form of countless discussions, had no greater efficacy than the stated intention of restoring balance-of-payments equilibrium.

Lastly, "mindful of the more distant future and the possibility that gold and reserve currency availabilities might be inadequate in relation to the aggregate needs of the world economy, the ministers and the governors approved the arrangements made by their alternates with a view to the setting up of a study group to examine the various proposals concerning the creation of reserve instruments through the IMF or otherwise."

For the purpose of implementing the above provisions, four international conferences were held: in Munich in April 1967, between the members of the European community only; in London and in Rio de Janeiro in August and September 1967 respectively; and in Stockholm in March 1968.

These conferences gradually established the scheme for the creation of new international liquidities, the so-called "special drawing rights."

The additional liquidities thus created are not a mere credit instrument, as would have been the wish of the French delegates, but nothing other than plain currency, because they are not subject to the reimbursement obligations initially attached to them. Special drawing rights can move practically with full freedom as between the member states and can be used in transactions with third parties, in particular with the International Monetary Fund, which can receive or lend them just as if they were foreign currency or gold. Furthermore, the creation of special drawing rights is not subject to the two prerequisites that the French delegation demanded: the restoration of balance-of-payments equilibrium in reserve currency countries, and an affirmative finding on the existence of a general liquidity shortage.

The negotiations were followed by a series of serious monetary disturbances that looked like so many succeeding stages of evolution: the devaluation of the pound in November 1967; the aggravation of the U.S. balance-of-payments deficit ($4 billion in 1967); the San Antonio Plan of 1 January 1968 for the restoration of

U.S. balance-of-payments equilibrium by means of very stringent trade restrictions; and in March 1968, restrictions on dollar convertibility and at the same time the termination of the gold pool, with the resulting emergence of a free price for gold, together with the continuing deficit of Britain's balance of payments.

# XIII

---

## NATHANAËL OR PAPER-GOLD

The progress of the negotiations toward creating the special drawing rights, against the dictates of the most elementary common sense, was viewed with anxiety by me. Therefore I deemed it necessary to warn public opinion about the dangers and hazards of the serious monetary disturbances involved in the policy that the Western nations seemed resigned to accept.

I made my position clear in an article published in *Le Monde* of 19 September 1967, under the above title:

The London solution, as a compromise between paper-gold, which the Americans wanted to create, and paper convertible into gold in accordance with French wishes, is beyond the purview of discursive reason and is only amenable to the appreciation of the negotiating parties. Considering all they knew and in particular the thoughts and afterthoughts that had occurred to them in the course of five years of fruitless ratiocinations, they were the only ones in a position consciously to choose between what was desirable and what was feasible.

But reason regains its rightful place the moment you have to predict and appreciate the consequences of the proposed reform.

During the ministerial meeting of 17–18 July 1967, the partici-
pants consistently affirmed and solemnly reaffirmed that any reform
would only be implemented once the U.S. balance-of-payments
deficit had been eliminated, failing which such reform would only
look like an expedient to enable the deficit to be settled for a little
while longer without any gold transfer.

There are two procedures—and only two—for correcting a
balance-of-payments deficit: either administrative action through
authoritative controls of capital outflows, or introduction of an
adequate money-management technique.

The continuation of the U.S. balance-of-payments deficit over
the past six years, notwithstanding the oft-repeated determination
of the U.S. Government to eliminate it, and the ever-renewed statement by the highest U.S. financial authorities that the deficit was
going to be eliminated, are proof positive that efforts to restore
equilibrium by manipulating the credit and debit sides of international trade are totally unavailing, except in totalitarian countries. If such efforts had been likely to yield the intended result,
that would have been assured in the United States, considering
the propitious nature of the quasi-insularity of the American
continent, the patriotic loyalty of its people, and the high technical
caliber of its economists.

Is it not a strange paradox that the country of free enterprise
should become the champion of a procedure that can achieve
relative efficacy only within the framework of authoritative structures and the strictest controls that smack of the police state?

It would be wrong to believe that the U.S. balance-of-payments
deficit is an inevitable consequence of the Vietnam war. France's
balance of payments was never more healthy than in the last period
of the Algerian war.

As to equilibrium brought about by influencing aggregate demand, that is, by relying on monetary policy, this can be achieved
either by the operation of the gold standard—in other words, by
the *de jure* or *de facto* elimination of the offsetting mechanisms
arising out of the gold-exchange standard—or by a credit policy
deliberately and consciously generating those contractions in pur-

chasing power which settlement in gold of the deficits would have brought about.

It goes without saying that the special drawing rights which are a new modality of the many expedients that have characterized international monetary policy since 1961 (general arrangements to borrow, swaps, Roosa bonds, IMF quota increases) will eliminate or mitigate the influences of a strictly monetary nature working toward restoration of equilibrium.

As regards the substitution of a conscious credit policy for the variations in aggregate demand that the gold standard would have brought about, the example of the United States shows once again that where the government had to take account of public opinion, this was not politically feasible.

It is therefore highly unlikely that, under the existing conditions, the U.S. balance-of-payments equilibrium can be restored in the near future. And there is no doubt that special drawing rights, if created notwithstanding the deficit, would prevent the restoration of such equilibrium.

## A VERY ODD DECISION

Nevertheless, the high monetary authorities of the United States, urged on by zealous mediators, state that "gold as an exchange instrument is bound to disappear" and want to substitute "paper-gold" instead.

The first reason, they say, is that "one does not see how enough gold could be made available to meet international payments requirements."

With the gold price at its present level, they are certainly right. But they forget that since the price of gold was fixed at this level ($35 an ounce) in 1934, all prices in the United States have more than doubled. Gold requirements are not related to a specific weight but to a specific value. The decision that maintained the price of the yellow metal at a level unrelated to the general price level has in fact reduced by more than 50 percent the nominal value of gold stocks and the value of annual gold production, compared to the levels they would have attained if computed in terms of a normal price.

Apart from this purely arithmetical consequence, the maintenance of the gold price at its 1934 level has reduced the volume of annual gold production because it has made gold mining, in particular in marginal mines, less remunerative than would have been the case if the price of gold had been maintained roughly at its rightful place in the price hierarchy.

To appreciate the significance of this consequence, one need only imagine what production of wheat would be if this commodity sold at its 1934 price.

In addition, the maintenance of the gold price at a level unrelated to all other prices eliminates the regulating influence which tends to adjust gold production to market requirements.

Lastly, the insufficient value that results for the U.S. gold stock from the present price of gold, compared with the level of dollar balances, gives rise to a feeling that, notwithstanding the ever-renewed statements of the U.S. Government, convertibility into gold might not be indefinitely guaranteed. Fears of a gold embargo obviously lead to a hoarding of gold, so much so that in 1965 the increase in total monetary reserves was only $250 million, as against $740 million in 1964 and $840 million in 1963. Furthermore, in 1966 official gold stocks, far from increasing, declined by about $90 million.

For the above reasons, the artificial pegging of the gold price at its 1934 level creates a shortage in the gold stock, a shortage in gold production, and a shortfall in that part of production which goes to increase the monetary reserves.

But this shortfall on three different counts is in no way inherent in the nature of things. It is fully and exclusively the effect of a very odd decision which has maintained the gold price at its 1934 level in a world where since that date prices in terms of gold have more than doubled as a result of a world war and of fifteen years of operation of the gold-exchange standard.

It goes without saying that such a decision might not have been made and could be rescinded at any time. It is therefore of an essentially contingent nature.

To state that special drawing rights must be created to offset a shortage of gold that has in fact been intentionally provoked amounts to repeating the (to say the least) irrational gesture of Gide's Nathanaël, who "was guided by the light that he carried in his own hand."

## NOTHINGNESS DRESSED UP AS CURRENCY

In the words of the London communiqué, special drawing rights are to be "a new facility to supplement existing reserve assets as and when the need may arise."

But the deflection of gold production from monetary reserves to hoarding, together with the "disengaging" of the regulating influence of newly mined gold through variations in the general price level, will undoubtedly lead to the need to "supplement existing assets."

There is more: the signs of an economic slowdown, which have become evident throughout the world since many countries have only reluctantly consented to increase their dollar balances, show that it is necessary to supplement existing assets.

The champions of the maintenance of the gold price at its 1934 level would be ill-inspired to shed any tears over the sufferings that a possible intensification of the recession might cause. Their moans and groans would sound very much like those of someone who has orphaned himself by murdering his own father and then implores compassion.

If, against all common sense, the present situation—I mean the pegging of the price of gold—lasts any longer, the creation of additional liquidity will surely become necessary. We are even given to understand that the United States would have wished the principle of the creation of an additional $1 billion to $2 billion every year to be accepted at this stage.

In the words of a high-placed American official, "There is no instrument more practical or more flexible . . . than an abstract exchange unit. It is just a matter of transposing onto the international plane the system applied everywhere for all internal transactions."

Flexible it will indeed be. The only thing to be feared is that it might be all too flexible, like the inconvertible currencies of which, alas, the world has long experience. Is there any reason to believe that the high authorities of the International Monetary Fund will, jointly, be wiser, more reasonable, more independent, and more alert to the situation than the national monetary authorities have so often been in the past?

As to the view that special drawing rights are akin to national currencies, this is fallacious. Except in times of runaway inflation, the national currencies have a counterpart in the assets of the bank of issue in the form of gold, commercial bills, warrants, promissory notes from solvent debtors, or Treasury bills that are the representation of future public revenue.

Special drawing rights, notwithstanding a by no means complete reimbursement clause, will only be nothingness dressed up as currency.

In the event that substantial quantities of drawing rights are created, they cannot but lead to total monetary inconvertibility. Thus, being a mere extension of the jaded dollar-balances policy in a new form, they will open the door wide to chronic inflation.

## ADVENTURE OR EXPANSION?

Whether or not they realize it, what inspires the keenest champions of the reform is fear of deflation. Like William Jennings Bryan, they do not want to "crucify mankind upon a cross of gold."

They forget, however, that the danger of inflation stems only from their refusal to envisage any change in the price of gold, which would bring about, without any inflation, a dehoarding of the yellow metal, a substantial and lasting decline in all interest rates, and a huge increase in investment possibilities—thereby bringing an assured wave of prosperity of considerable magnitude and long duration.

Thus, for those who want the world to enjoy prosperity and well-being, the choice is a simple one. We shall have either a reckless scheme in the form of a paper-gold system that will suffer the fate of all inconvertible currencies, or expansion within stability through the deliberate restoration of a system of gold convertibility purged of all those deviations which until now have impaired its durability.

Let us hope that the creation of special drawing rights, if the conditions to which it is subject are ever met, will not unduly delay a return—which in any case will come to pass—to order, stability, and common sense.

# XIV

## AN ECONOMIC HERESY:
## THE FEEDBACK SCHEME FOR
## EXPORTED CAPITAL

The preceding pages show how indifferent expert committees and meetings of ministers or governors were to the doctrinal basis for their action.

It is certainly a good thing, and a sound thing too, to act in a practical way, provided however that the action undertaken does not produce results contrary to those that were sought. Such would undoubtedly have been the outcome of a strange scheme that was seriously considered during the latter part of 1968 and is still being envisaged by some experts who are more anxious to act than to secure efficacious results.

The scheme is so markedly unreasonable that it is worth examining, although it has until now remained a dead letter, because it shows what misconceptions can result from intellectual exercises that are not supported by proven economic theories.

I made my position clear regarding the economic heresy inherent in the feedback scheme for exported capital in an article that appeared in *Le Figaro* of 12 December 1968 and was reproduced in the *Financial Times,* the *Frankfurter Allgemeine Zeitung, La Libre Belgique,* the Spanish paper *Madrid,* the

*Mainichi Shimbum* of Tokyo, *Eleptheros Kosmos* in Athens, and *The Globe* and *Mail* in Toronto:

Press reports indicate that the governors of the central banks at their meeting in Basel on 8 and 9 December discussed a scheme for the feedback of exported capital, i.e., its return to the country of origin through the extension of loans or the subscription of Treasury bills.

I can hardly believe that this is true. I have too much confidence in the profound conscientiousness of the men to whom such a scheme is ascribed to imagine that they have deliberately engaged upon such a dangerous course.

But this piece of news is substantiated by subsequent facts that cannot possibly be doubted. Paragraph 8 of the official communiqué issued at the end of the meeting of the Ten held in Bonn on 23 November 1963 reads as follows:

> The decision concerning credit facilities emphasizes the determination of the monetary authorities . . . to off-set the destabilizing influence of short-term capital in-flows on the reserves. To this end, the governors, in cooperation with the Bank for International Settlements, are considering new arrangements with the Central Banks to mitigate the impact of speculative moves on the reserves.

Such statements are borne out by an item of news announcing that "the Secretary of the U.S. Treasury in his press conference of Tuesday, 26 November 1968, launched the idea of an international scheme to neutralize capital movements."

Thus, the least one can say is that the idea of the feedback is in the air, and is even courted with a great deal of sympathy by some high officials who are reported to view it as a means to ward off speculative movements of capital.

But we must be very careful. The feedback of exported capital is the art of sending it back to the economy where it originated, and therefore of nullifying the credit shrinkage that tends to result from the export of capital in the markets of those countries where it originated. It is therefore the art of making possible the indefinite continuation of speculative movements of capital by systematically offsetting the credit constriction that inevitably results and that would have tended to put an end to such moves, had it been allowed to take place.

It is the art of institutionalizing, and therefore of turning into a widespread and permanent feature, the policy followed by France—not, of course, with evil intentions, but as a result of the practices and traditions that characterize the French money market. What France did was to replace, between 2 May and 21 November 1968, the 17.1 billion francs of capital that had been exported by 23.3 billion francs of newly created credit, thus nullifying the influence that could and should have put an end to the capital outflows by drying up their sources.

Lastly, it is the art of bringing about in creditor countries an indefinite accumulation of short-term claims, which are akin to dollar and sterling balances and are bound to impair beyond remedy the solvency of the debtor country and to cause the type of disturbance that their volatile nature has inflicted upon the currencies of the United States and Britain.

The feedback is, after all, a mere device to eliminate the effects without eradicating the causes. Clearly one could only expect such a strange word to conceal a strange gimmick, good, at best, for amusing children.

I hope that this proposed scheme will not only be turned down, but also finally rejected, together with all schemes tending to spare a capital-exporting country the credit shrinkage that must ensue from, and is the only remedy to, capital exports.

I hope that the governors of the banks of issue will spare the community of Western nations a repetition of France's transgression when she offset, by the creation of credit, the restricting effect of capital outflows.

I hope that they will advise the future victims of capital exports not only to allow them to occur but to intensify, to the greatest extent possible, the credit constriction and the rise in interest rates, the only factors that can put an end to their ordeals.

The problem is a grave one. The Western nations are on the verge of monetary catastrophe. Let us at least ensure that new expedients do not precipitate its onset or increase the scope and magnitude of the tribulations and sufferings that it will, alas, inevitably bring in its wake.

---

# "We Shall Have the Consequences"

The words that serve as the title for Part Four of this book are taken from the epigraph to one of Jacques Bainville's books, which deals with "the economic consequences of peace."[1] This phrase, says Bainville, is to be found in Ecclesiastes, where it is supplemented by another, purporting to convey the same message: "He that diggeth a pit shall fall into it" (Ecclesiastes X8).

These two quotations set the tone, so to speak, for the following three chapters. They are devoted to a study of "the consequences" and, alas, bring out their implacable unfolding.

Yet this is not quite the right phrase. We have the consequences already, and I intend to show how considerable they are.

[1] *Les conséquences économiques de la paix* (Paris: Nouvelle Librairie Nationale, 1920).

# XV

---

## A TREND THAT CANNOT
## BE REVERSED

The creation of special drawing rights signaled a trend in international monetary policy that could not be reversed: the inflationary trend with which we had decided to drift, like a dead dog drifting with the current.

The period that followed the September 1967 IMF meeting in Rio de Janeiro witnessed the first manifestations of the total disruption of the international monetary system. These were the devaluation of the pound in November 1967; an estimated $4 billion deficit for the U.S. balance of payments; restrictions on dollar convertibility, mainly in pursuance of the San Antonio Plan of 1 January 1968 (see page 153); the liquidation of the gold pool and the emergence of a two-tier gold market on 17 March 1968; the amendment, on the same date, of the rules and practices for convertibility of the dollar into gold as a result of a meeting of the Board of Governors hastily convened in Washington; the continuing deficit of Britain's balance of payments.

Obviously we were right in the middle of a monetary storm. From then on, there could be no question of uttering words of caution. The only hope we could have was that a thorough examination would at last bring out the true causes of the evil and pave the way for the preparation of appropriate remedies.

At the end of April 1968, I wrote a "Letter to American Friends" at the request of a well-known American magazine. I endeavored to show that the San Antonio Program under which President Johnson on 1 January 1968 had imposed a whole range of authoritative measures to restore balance-of-payments equilibrium would be unavailing and was doomed to failure.

The serious disturbances that jolted France in May 1968 did not allow me to carry out this project. The text was not completed and was never published. It is reproduced here, however, because it provides some insight into the ingredients of the San Antonio Program. Also, in regard to subsequent U.S. balance-of-payments developments, it enables one to assert again the impossibility of restoring the U.S. balance-of-payments equilibrium through administrative manipulations. It was important that this lesson should not be lost to history.

## LETTER TO AMERICAN FRIENDS

Dear friends,

Many of you look on my monetary reform proposal as being an anti-American undertaking. Do you really believe that I can possibly forget the circumstances in which on two different occasions in my life I was in contact with the American army: in March 1918 on the Château-Thierry front, and in August 1944 in the Rhône valley. I have also witnessed the efforts and sacrifices made by your great country to nurse the wounds that the war had left in Europe. These are memories which preclude any possibility of hostile or even unfriendly feelings on my part toward the United States.

I know what are the origin and the aims of the thoughts I express in the monetary field. I know that, far from being in the service of national interests, they are intended to restore economic order in the Western community of nations and more specifically in the United States and Britain, which are the main victims of the existing monetary system.

I would hope to convince you once and for all that this is really the case.

Your balance of payments has been in deficit since 1950. But you had such substantial gold reserves that your gold losses left you totally indifferent. It was only after President Kennedy took office that your government began to pay attention to the problem, as is evidenced by the President's message of 6 February 1961.

Since then, you have often stated your firm resolve to restore the balance of your external commitments. One of your high financial authorities was telling me in 1962: "We have not only a program but also a schedule. The deficit will be reduced by half at the end of 1962 and will have been fully eliminated by the end of 1963." You know what actually happened.

You were relying on a reduction of your foreign expenditure to restore your balance-of-payments equilibrium. Thus, in 1965 you invented the concept of "self-restraint" and requested your nationals to eliminate or restrain their external commitments.

This policy blossomed out into the program announced by President Johnson at San Antonio on 1 January 1968, which comprises a set of regulations and draft legislation with a view to limiting your direct investments abroad through governmental measures, and imposing varying and therefore discriminatory quotas in respect of Western European countries, other developed countries, and developing countries. Under the program, U.S. undertakings are required to repatriate profits made or accumulated overseas; purchases of foreign stocks and shares by American citizens are subject to a 15 percent equalization tax; loans abroad are restricted; American citizens are requested—though not as yet required—to refrain from making any nonessential journeys abroad during the next two years. In addition, a reduction is to be made in foreign-exchange expenditure by American military personnel and their families stationed outside the United States, the Allies of the United States are called upon to increase their armaments purchases and long-term investments in the United States, and subsidization is envisaged for American exports as well as for foreign investments and tourism in the United States.

We in Europe are familiar with all these measures, having suffered and applied them for many years. Beyond any doubt, they
constitute exchange-control measures.

We know full well that, if they are to be effective, most stringent
administrative controls must be imposed in various fields and
the powers and the number of the officials responsible for their
implementation must be greatly augmented. Can the country that
is the home of free enterprise really accept such a course?

But if the present gives cause for anxiety, the future is more
disquieting still. Dr. Schacht's controls were also initially modest.
The logic of the system, if it is intended to preclude inequality
and disorder, inevitably requires an increasing degree of inter-
ference in economic life. In the words of my eminent friend
Robert Roosa, former Undersecretary of the U.S. Treasury:[1]

> To try to impose controls over outward capital move-
> ments in any one sector of these markets—say, bank
> loans—would only invite capital flight through many
> others, and to try instead a comprehensive approach—
> clamping the cold hand of capital issues controls, or
> credit rationing, over the entire sweep of the markets
> —would literally congeal the bloodstream of American
> capitalism.

The consequences upon the international relations of the United
States will be serious. Under the pretext of safeguarding the balance of payments, the United States has already brought into
question some of the military expenditure abroad, in particular
expenditure resulting from the stationing of American forces in
Germany. The political consequences of an appreciable reduction
in the strength maintained abroad will be no less than those of
Britain's withdrawal from Singapore ahead of schedule for balance-of-payments reasons.

[1] Quoted in "U.S. Balance of Payments Policies and International Monetary
Reform," by Gottfried Haberler and Thomas Willett, American Enterprise
Institute for Public Policy Research, September 1968, p. 17.

The United States, however, will not be the only country affected. The intensification of U.S. protection against foreign imports in all sectors, and the subsidization of exports will give rise—as was the case in 1931—to retaliatory measures and probably also to the reestablishment of import quotas or prohibitions.

If the dollar were to be devalued unilaterally—which no government can hope for, and least of all the French Government—the increased competitiveness of U.S. goods would cause a profound disruption of international trade flows. The benefits derived from the liberalization of trade that has been tenaciously pursued for the past twenty years would be lost, together with the great increase in the peoples' standard of living that has resulted.

At the same time, the measures introduced in the United States to control exports of capital will force American undertakings in Europe to borrow in local markets. Interest rates, already quite high, may well reach prohibitive levels. Does anyone believe that it is possible to maintain prosperity and, *a fortiori,* expansion in the face of long-term borrowing rates of 7½ percent?[2] No one can possibly doubt that the present credit situation, if it continues, will lead to recession and unemployment.

Thus, endeavors to check the U.S. balance-of-payments deficit through direct controls threaten the economic civilization from which the Western community of nations has derived its prosperity and well-being. We should heed Mr. Brezhnev's warning of 29 March 1968, when he declared: "After the devaluation of the pound, we are now witnessing the beginning of the devaluation of the United States dollar, and in such circumstances the possibility of a profound crisis of the capitalist system should not be excluded."

Is it really the mission of the country that has best safeguarded the free play of market forces for the greatest benefit of its people and of the community of Western nations to sound the death knell of the civilization from which it has derived its prosperity and matchless grandeur?

[2] Since this was written, interest rates have reached substantially higher levels.

The measures included in the program of 1 January 1968 could nevertheless be condoned if they were to remedy the ills besetting the dollar, in other words, if they were to restore U.S. balance-of-payments equilibrium.

Clearly, no one can imagine that this could happen. The remedy that such measures afford is based exclusively on the notion that a balance of payments is an aggregate of independent components and that it suffices to reduce one item of liabilities in order to reduce by a corresponding amount the net deficit in international exchanges.

This view is reminiscent of the concept that saw in the dollar gap of the 1945–1958 period a structural phenomenon resulting from Europe's inability to find a means of equilibrating its foreign exchanges within its economic structures, which were supposed to have been provided once and for all by a niggardly Nature.

Now, the moment the great nations of the West terminated their inflationary postwar policies, their deficits that had been regarded as structural gave way to surpluses, and the dollar gap, to a dollar glut.

This thoroughgoing change is proof positive that balance-of-payments components are not a natural endowment, but are determined by aggregate demand phenomena that make them interdependent and control their variations with extreme sensitivity and precision.

In any case, economic theory and a great many precedents show that, all things being equal, the elimination of a liabilities item will necessarily reduce not the balance-of-payments deficit, but the trade surplus where there is one, as is the case with the United States.[3]

If it had been possible to restore balance-of-payments equilibrium through administrative controls, the United States, with the efficiency of its administration and the loyalty of its people, would

---

[3] I have mentioned a number of examples in a recent publication, *Balance of Payments* (New York: Macmillan 1967), which show beyond question the futility of any efforts tending to shape the balance of payments by means of administrative measures.

have succeeded in doing so. It is clear, however, that notwithstanding its efforts, this has not been achieved.

It would be wrong to contend that the deficit is the result of the Vietnam war effort. This deficit existed before the Vietnam war, and if there is no reform of the monetary system the deficit will continue after the war has been ended. During the Algerian conflict, France had a large external payments deficit until December 1958 and a considerable surplus thereafter when, notwithstanding the continuation of the war, it restored efficacious monetary management at home.

The reemergence of inflationary situations in major non-American Western countries would, *a contrario,* tend to put their balance of payments in deficit, thereby restoring equilibrium in the U.S. balance of payments.[4]

This experience shows that one can rest assured that the components of any balance of payments cannot be considered independent from one another and that the elimination of items of liabilities must often result, *ceteris paribus,* in a deterioration of the trade balance rather than an improvement of the balance of payments.

In any case, there are no grounds for believing that the administrative manipulations introduced under the 1 January 1968 program will restore U.S. balance-of-payments equilibrium. The adverse effects that such manipulations will generate for the United States and, thereby, for the entire Western economy will not restore equilibrium in international trade. Such efforts will prove unavailing and unnecessary.

---

[4] Such a situation was effectively observed during the few weeks that followed the May 1968 disturbances in France.

# XVI

---

## WHAT IS TO BE, WILL BE[1]

On 17 March 1968, the international monetary system exploded. Yet public opinion was not convinced that the mutation that had occurred was the unavoidable consequence of previous transgressions of the dictates of common sense in selecting the rules to govern monetary convertibility. This "fatal blemish" was most grave because it prevented any effective reconstruction effort.

As soon as the monetary storm that lasted throughout 1968 had subsided, I thought it necessary to bring to light the links between cause and effect and to show once again, on this occasion, that you can never be sure you have seen the worst, and what is unavoidable is usually nothing but what you have been unable or unwilling to avoid.

This led to the publication in *Le Monde* on 4, 5, and 6 June 1969 of the three articles reproduced here, which appeared under the above title.[2]

---

1 *Und wie es gehn kann, so wird's gehn*, Goethe, *Faust* I.
2 These articles were published on the same dates by the *Frankfurter Allgemeine Zeitung, La Libre Belgique,* the *Wall Street Journal, Asahi Shimbum,* the *Naftemporiky* in Athens, the *South African Daily News,* and various other daily papers.

## 1. THE LAST TWITCHES OF THE INTERNATIONAL MONETARY SYSTEM

People often tell me, "You have been warning ever since 1961 about the dangers that threaten the international monetary system. Yet nothing has happened."

I would not challenge this judgment if it merely cast doubt on the relevance of my own judgment. But the validity of the premises on which my forecasts were based is also being challenged, and therefore the remedies I recommended are being questioned.

For this reason I feel obliged to show that for eight years the sequence of events has followed the path I predicted. Nearly everything that I forecast has come to pass. Only the final act is still pending, but it will be the most formidable one.

My analysis predicted consequences that did in fact follow. Recognition of this will add credibility, I hope, to those predictions that are as yet unfulfilled. More important, this substantiation should bring about the inception of a policy designed to avoid the grave difficulties that will ensue if nothing is done to stem the onrushing course of events.

Any deficit in a country's balance of payments means that some of this debtor country's money is paid to a creditor country.

The gold standard was in use throughout the world until 1922, and then again from 1933 to 1940. Under this system, a bank of issue cannot create money that is not backed by gold or other claims—such as commercial bills or treasury bills—denominated in the currency of that country. For this reason, as soon as a bank of issue holds more foreign exchange than it needs for current settlements, the bank requests the debtor country to pay gold from its reserves for the undesired exchange in its vaults. This surplus is thus siphoned off and the debt to the creditor that it represented is also extinguished.

A different system is the gold-exchange standard, which existed in a number of European countries between 1922 and 1930 and then again starting in 1945. Banks of issue may issue currency not only against gold and claims denominated in that currency, but also against foreign exchange payable in gold, in other words, against dollars.[3] Thus, when a central bank receives dollars in settlement of a balance-of-payments surplus, instead of cashing them in for gold, those dollars are included in the balance sheet.

But these dollars cannot be spent—if we disregard the existence of Eurodollars for the time being—in Bonn, Milan, or Brussels. Consequently, the bank that receives them invests them the same day in the form of bank deposits or treasury bonds in the New York money market. These dollars are not reabsorbed, and what is more, they represent for the bank of the lending country a claim to U.S. gold.

I predicted in 1961 that this system would inevitably lead to three types of consequences:

—A persistent deficit in the U.S. balance of payments as long as the aggregate credit supply was not deliberately and systematically contracted as the gold standard would have done automatically from day to day, hence imperceptibly

—Inflation in the creditor countries without any compensating deflation in the debtor country, causing prices to slide upward throughout the monetary convertibility area

—The ultimate disruption of the international monetary system by the growing insolvency of the dollar resulting from the unending accumulation of foreign "dollar balances" that constitute foreign claims, and by the ensuing widespread inflation

I also pointed out that if foreigners requested payment in gold for a substantial part of their dollar holdings, they could really bring about a collapse of the credit structure in the United States. They certainly would not do so, I added; but the mere fact that

---

[3] The pound sterling plays the same role as the dollar inside the sterling area. But to simplify, I will focus here on the problems of the dollar area.

they have the right to do it forces us to recall that it was the collapse of the house of cards built on the gold-exchange standard that turned the recession of 1929 into a Great Depression.

I concluded by affirming: "In 1960, the same circumstances are present, although on a different scale. Unless we watch out carefully, the same causes could produce the same effects." I went on: "It is absolutely necessary, before it's too late, to correct the situation resulting from the dual pyramidal structure based on the world gold stock."

Yet nothing has been done to correct the accumulating dollar balances since I made those predictions. On the contrary, the various committees that have been convened to cure the ailment have never ceased recommending makeshift solutions that have only aggravated it.

Thus, the general arrangements to borrow, swap agreements, Roosa bonds, increased quotas in the International Monetary Fund —all these have increased the holdings by non-Americans of American liquidities, which can be designated by the general term "dollar balances." Finally, this system blossomed into the indiscriminate, preposterous, and monstrous oversupply of Eurodollars, which gravely endangers the stability of the entire Western world.

### WHAT HAS HAPPENED AND WHAT HAD BEEN FORESEEN

Such is the system that people say has had no consequences until now. The only reply is to compare what has occurred and what had been foreseen.

### The Perpetual Deficit of the U.S. Balance of Payments

Despite endlessly renewed statements by the U.S. Government, its annual balance of foreign payments has remained in deficit almost constantly since 1958.

This trend seems to have leveled off in 1968. But this improvement was the result of temporary factors, such as restricted exports of capital from the United States, and especially the contributions by French students, with their disorders a years ago,

and by Mr. Brezhnev, with the Soviet occupation of Czechoslo-
vakia, which frightened capital toward the United States. But at
the start of 1969 it seems that these influences have abated. The
huge amounts of money siphoned off the Eurodollar market by
American banks show that the U.S. balance of payments is still
heavily in deficit.

### INFLATION IN CREDITOR COUNTRIES

Prices and especially hourly wages are rising faster than productivity. That clearly underscores the inflationary nature of the
economic situation in most Western countries, and there is no
need for supporting data.

This trend developed without the United States experiencing a
credit shrink such as would have resulted, under the gold standard,
from its balance-of-payments deficit. Nor did the Federal Reserve Banks try to create deflationary trends by restricting credit,
as the deficit would have done if the gold-exchange standard had
not been in operation.

As a result of a foreseeable inducement process, the inflationary
trends in the rest of the world, in the absence of any deflationary
tendencies in the United States, gradually spread to the American
market. Thus price levels in Western countries have been lifted
by a powerful inflationary wave which, as is usually the case, has
been accompanied by an unprecedented boom.

### DISRUPTION OF THE SYSTEM

The disruption of the system appears in every aspect of the
free world's monetary situation as the outcome of the growing
accumulation of foreign claims on the U.S. gold stock—a characteristic of the gold-exchange standard—and of inflationary movements in most Western countries, as well as the credit restrictions
recently introduced by the United States in an attempt to control
the consequences of such movements.

The most unmistakable proof of this disruption is the recurrence of major monetary crises resulting from short-term capital shifts. These have upset international economic relations in the last few years. The most spectacular crises were probably those sparked by rumors that the mark was going to be revalued in November 1968 and May 1969. It has been stated that on 9 May alone, $1.3 billion moved into Germany.

Under the gold standard, Germany could not have kept this foreign exchange among the assets of its central bank and would have been obliged to ask the United States to exchange it for gold. The dollars thus reimbursed would simply have been mopped up. There is no doubt that the resulting constriction of credit would have caused this tidal wave of foreign capital flooding Germany to subside from lack of funds to sustain it.

But the rules of the gold-exchange standard authorized Germany to include these dollars among the assets of the Bundesbank. In addition, it was forced to do so by pressure from the United States, on whom it depends for its military defense. Germany, therefore, did not exercise its right to claim gold. Thus, there was no credit shrink in the United States, and capital shifts could continue as long as the speculative hopes that had prompted them persisted.

In the above case, the process was further complicated and compounded by the existence of the very unstable mass of funds that the Eurodollar market represents. The German monetary authorities wished to get rid of their surplus dollars discreetly without antagonizing the United States. So part of them were loaned to German banks, which invested them in the Eurodollar market. "But this method turned out to be very dangerous in the last three weeks," wrote Paul Fabra in *Le Monde* on 11 May, "because the funds thus shifted back home were immediately reused to buy more deutschmarks, thereby giving new impetus to the speculative move." Obviously, speculation could not have gone on if Germany had used its right to purchase gold from the United States, thus simply mopping up the dollars sent abroad.

The accumulation of dollar claims increased cumulated dollar balances from $15 billion in 1958 to about $35 billion at the end of 1968. True, during the same period, certain holders of dollar balances exercised their right—sometimes by devious means—to obtain gold, although this was frowned upon by the United States. This caused the U.S. gold stock to decline from $23 billion to $11 billion.

Simple juxtaposition of these figures underscores that reimbursing the gold claims that encumber the dollar has become not only impossible, but inconceivable, notwithstanding the immense power of the American economy.

I know that this view will come as a surpise to those who are aware of the wealth of the American continent. Let them remember, however, that sight liabilities are met out of foreign-exchange holdings, not out of investments, and that banking catastrophes nearly always result from a shortage of liquidy rather than from lack of assets.

## THE THIRST FOR TANGIBLES

Under present conditions, no sensible person can expect that owners of dollar balances will wait, undismayed, until the only liquid assets that are the counterpart of their claims vanish. Theirs has been a natural reaction, perfectly foreseeable and quite in keeping with all known precedents. They tried to cash in their claim by requesting gold or tangible assets before the dollar's convertibility into gold was suspended, as happened on 18 March 1968—an unavoidable occurrence, considering the volume of U.S. indebtedness.

The thirst for tangibles or gold, i.e., the refusal to hold on to claims denominated in currency, was amplified by the spreading of inflationary trends resulting from the U.S. balance-of-payments deficit, or from local conditions like those caused in France by the May–June 1968 disturbances and their aftermath.

Of course, interest rates tend to decrease at the beginning of inflationary periods because there is an abundant supply of money. But when the feeling spreads that claims denominated in currency are only reimbursable in a currency that is bound to depreciate, then acceptance of such claims tapers off, whereas requests for reimbursement of claims previously accepted are stepped up.

It was requests for gold and tangibles by holders of currency resources that caused the first changes that are so characteristic of the disruption of the international monetary system.

This is evidenced by the establishment of a two-tier gold market in March 1968, with gold selling at the official price of $35 an ounce on the one hand and being freely negotiated at $43.5 an ounce on the other.[4] It is also evidenced by the strict currency controls set up in Britain and France, the severe restrictions on capital exports from the United States, the exorbitant interest rates of 8 or 9 percent—and often more—prevailing in the main monetary and financial markets, and the very significant inversion in the ratio between dividend and interest rates in major financial markets.

It can be observed that requests for gold, which were mainly responsible for these self-defense measures, come from the Zurich "gnomes," who are prompted by sordid motivations. But the reply to this is to be found in the First National City Bank of New York's bulletin of January 1969, which stresses that the official gold reserves of Germany, Italy, Belgium, The Netherlands, Switzerland, Portugal, and various other countries increased by a total of $2,027 million from April to September 1968. "The fact that so many governments and central banks did not miss the chance to increase their reserves of monetary gold, shows once again," the bulletin concludes, "the deep desire of monetary authorities to own such reserves."

Besides, most major countries confirm that desire "by keeping 60 to 90 percent of their reserves in the form of gold."

The significance of these figures appears most fully when one notices that the gold component in the monetary reserves of the world is diminishing at the same time. Gold reserves declined from $40.8 billion in late 1964 to $38.7 billion last September, according to a report by Professor Triffin. Apparently hoarding of the yellow

4 At the time of writing, i.e., in May 1969.

metal not only absorbed the new output of mines, but also removed $2 billion from world monetary reserves. This contraction seems particularly serious when compared with the trade expansion that characterized the same period.

The quest for tangibles, gold, real estate, and works of art, which is the inevitable counterpart of reducing cash holdings or assets denominated in currency to a minimum, accounts for all the features of the monetary disruption developing before our eyes.

In view of these deep disturbances, who dares maintain that the grave difficulties forecast in 1961 never materialized? Alas, the first four acts of the drama have been performed already. Only the fifth is yet to come. But it will certainly come, and it will be a tragic act if nothing is done to avoid it.

Nobody can question that interest rates of 8 or 9 percent are totally incompatible with the generous and enthusiastic investment policy that is a *sine qua non* for enduring economic growth. There is no doubt that such rates cannot continue and that, under present conditions, they will cause the economy to reach a plateau, then decline steeply.

One can only shudder when pointing out that the U.S. discount rate is 6 percent, a level it had reached before only for a few months at the end of 1929; and that in England it is 8 percent. Is it possible in this field that the same causes, if they continue, cannot eventually have the same effects?

Evoking the dangers that threaten is sacrilege, in the eyes of some people. They would be right if we were condemned to await disaster passively. Luckily, that is not the case. If these dangers come to pass, they will only be the result of ignorance and inaction. It is an overriding obligation for all those watching the steadily growing perils to denounce them and untiringly request measures to remove from our path the certainty of another Great Depression.

Such remedies exist. They are simple and well proven, and only require farsightedness, courage, and determination.

In the next two sections, I propose to show what are the two alternatives open to us. I shall endeavor to assess the chances of success of the two solutions, in the hope that before it is too late, the monetary authorities in Western nations will endorse a proposed reform that would safely and promptly restore, without any adverse effects, those conditions that are the prerequisite to economic stability and social progress.

## 2. SPECIAL DRAWING RIGHTS

The exorbitant rise in interest rates implies grave dangers for Western prosperity. If we want to stop it, the only solution is to eradicate the cause.

The preceding article showed that the cause lay wholly in the fact that those who own funds dislike investments in money, such as short-, medium-, or long-term loans or bonds.

Rather than invest in money, they prefer acquiring tangible goods, gold, land, houses, corporate shares, paintings, and other works of art having an intrinsic value because of their scarcity or the demand for them.

This preference for tangible goods over assets denominated in currency stems from a feeling that currencies that are all linked to the dollar *de facto* or *de jure* are likely, if not certain, to depreciate as a result of the growing insolvency of the two reserve currencies, the dollar and the pound. It is also due to the degree of inflation prevailing in many countries in the Western world.

There is only one way to sweep away the somber clouds that block our economic horizon, and that is to promptly restore these two reserve currencies to unquestioned international solvency and to eradicate the sources of inflation arising from overliberal credit policies or from special circumstances like those which, in France, followed the disturbances of May–June 1968. Restoring international solvency of the dollar and the pound means ensuring that the United States and Britain can meet without any limitation any request for reimbursement of dollar and sterling balances or any other claims denominated in those currencies.

To that end, two sets of solutions have been proposed: those based on the creation *ex nihilo* of new monetary resources and those implying an increase in the price of gold.

As regards the first type, various plans have been drawn up. The Triffin plan is the oldest one, while the most elaborate is the "special drawing rights" scheme that has been submitted for ratification to the member governments of the Western monetary community of nations.

These projects have one feature in common: they provide for the creation, by various means, of a new international currency that is defined in terms of gold, but is not reimbursable in gold.

This currency can be issued in limited quantity and can be used by debtor countries to settle their balance-of-payments deficits. Thus, claims that creditor countries wanted to convert will be substituted by this new monetary instrument, which is definitely not convertible into gold.

## "UNEARNED" MONEY

Issuing procedures differ from one scheme to another. I shall concentrate on the procedure to be followed in the case of special drawing rights.

Each country participating in this scheme will receive an allocation of special drawing rights annually. Within the limits of that allocation, the country may ask the International Monetary Fund to deliver whatever foreign currency is needed to settle its balance-of-payments deficits or any other currency or currencies through which the currency needed can be purchased.

A country requesting the IMF to provide currencies to settle a deficit will use up a corresponding amount of drawing rights in the fund. Conversely, a country contributing to the fund the currency used for such settlement will be credited with a corresponding increase in its special drawing-rights entitlement.

Such a transaction will reduce a debtor's means of international payment and increase those of a creditor. In appearance, the transaction will very much look as if settlement had been effected by transferring gold. Special drawing rights will really look like "paper-gold."

But that is only an illusion. In reality, there are profound differences between payment in gold and payment in special drawing rights:

a. Gold is mined from the earth or acquired through balance-of-payments surpluses. In either case, it is consideration for a productive effort by the community that receives it.

By contrast, special drawing rights will be created from scratch as a result of a discretionary decision by the International Monetary Fund.

b. It can be argued that this distribution of money will not be inequitable, because all countries can benefit in proportion to their quotas in the International Monetary Fund.

But in the circumstances, equality will only be theoretical. The facility of using special drawing rights for purchases abroad will be reserved for countries with balance-of-payments deficits. Unless a country attains the blessed state of having a deficit, it cannot use its drawing rights, not even to buy gold for its industry or to modify the composition of its reserves.

This is the main difference between gold and special drawing rights. The former provides unconditional buying power that is subject to the sole sovereignty of its owner. The latter is a conditional facility to purchase abroad, which is subject to the discretionary—hence political—appreciation of the issuing body.

Under the plan being ratified, the amount of special drawing rights created annually is to be set once and for all for a period of five years. Each country receives an allocation proportional to its quota in the International Monetary Fund.

Thus gold is "earned," whereas special drawing rights are "allocated."

The impact of this difference can be measured by observing the ensuing consequences for a country whose gold and foreign exchange reserves fall too low.

Under the gold standard, the choice is simple. The country must either cease payments abroad or acquire the necessary means for international payments. If the second alternative is chosen, the country concerned either has to produce more gold or run a balance-of-payments surplus. In either case, means of payment abroad are obtained by giving up tangible goods, in other words, by consuming less real wealth at home. The "foreign purchasing power" thus obtained is strictly limited to the extent of the sacrifice in domestic consumption consented to. No clever scheme or political pressure can change this one whit.

By contrast, with the special drawing rights, the restoration of purchasing power abroad is only the outcome of an unrequited gift, which does not involve any sacrifice whatsoever on the part of the receiving country and depends on the discretion of the entity controlling the drawing rights, that is, in the case under consideration, the IMF.

The criterion that there can be no SDR entitlement unless a balance-of-payments deficit has been found to exist appears to be particularly dangerous if one considers how difficult and uncertain it is to assess a balance-of-payments outcome. Such assessments can vary widely, depending on the method of calculation, as shown by U.S. official statistics.

c. As regards a creditor country, the difference between gold and special drawing rights is just as great. When a creditor country receives gold, there is in fact an exchange between the goods delivered by the creditor country and the gold transferred by the debtor country. On the other hand, when a country receives special drawing rights, that country relinquishes a quantity of its own money, that is, a certain amount of purchasing power that could be exercised in the national territory in exchange for an asset created out of nothing, which will not become purchasing power in its particular case until and unless it runs a balance-of-payments deficit. In other words, a country receiving SDR's affords the debtor country the possibility of taking up some of its national production in exchange for a bare hope of being able to buy goods abroad some day, if the International Monetary Fund permits, and provided it has been "wise" enough to run a deficit.

The amount of money created in favor of the debtor country

will find its way home and increase the amount of money in circulation in the creditor country, which could be adversely affected, to the extent that it could have to introduce, sooner or later, monetary curbs or even a "stabilization plan."

## THE PRIVILEGE OF THE UNITED STATES

d. The preceding remarks become fully meaningful if one considers that the proposed agreement provides that a state "may utilize special drawing rights to avoid variations in its gross reserves."

That cryptic phrase has a very precise meaning. It means that the United States can use its special drawing rights to meet demands to convert dollar balances, even if its balance of payments in the usual sense is not in deficit.

When they accepted that clause, creditor countries assumed responsibility for reimbursing dollar balances in their own currencies if and when such reimbursement is requested.

When one considers how carefully spending commitments are controlled in every country, in particular through parliamentary procedures, one is amazed at the frivolousness with which this transfer of actual responsibility from debtor to creditor was agreed to.

e. The allocation of special drawing rights will obviously be limited to the maximum authorized each year by the International Monetary Fund. That amount is to be set for a period of five years.

In 1967, the U.S. Government estimated that it would be necessary to create the equivalent of $5 billion to $10 billion in SDR's over a period of five years. Today, nobody speaks of less than $10 billion and some want $15 billion.

Special drawing rights will be allocated in proportion to the quota of each member country in the International Monetary Fund. Considering that its quota amounts to 20 percent, the United States, on the assumption that the fund decided to issue a total amount of $10 billion in five years, would receive 20 percent of $2 billion dollars, or $400 million each year. This figure is ridiculously small in regard to the U.S. deficit, which over the past eleven years has averaged $2,300 million a year.

To be sure, the ceiling can be got around by numerous ancillary procedures. But whatever these may be, one cannot help being struck by the absence of any objective criterion for determining the amount of special drawing rights issued annually. The amount will be very important for debtor countries, especially the major reserve-currency debtor countries, the United States and Britain. In addition, the amount will be determined in a discretionary way. One can therefore easily imagine the political pressures that will be exerted in order that the amount issued should be as high as possible.

Any international monetary crisis, any major outflow of capital, to the extent that they affect powerful countries, will provide an opportunity for an inflationary issue of SDR's. This in turn will lead to powerful surges of inflation in creditor countries and subsequently over the rest of the world.

Thus the creation of special drawing rights, far from allaying fears of inflation, can only aggravate such fears, which at present exacerbate the unwillingness to hold assets denominated in money and the corresponding demand for tangible goods.

Of course, the creation of SDR's when it first becomes effective will ease interest rates by expanding the money supply. But the easing of interest rates will be a fleeting phenomenon, as is the case in every period of nascent inflation. The public will quickly realize that the special-drawing-rights solution is by nature inflationary. Rising prices must ensue, and people will seek protection against this very soon. Unwillingness to hold money and preference for tangibles will be accentuated. As is the case at present, this will stimulate exorbitant interest rates, which the reform was intended to prevent.

Taking into consideration these characteristics and inherent hazards, I do not believe that the special-drawing-rights scheme can afford a durable solution, or one broad enough to cope with monetary disturbances at present affecting the community of convertible-currency countries.

The SDR scheme will probably be accepted. Governments will "play at special drawing rights" for a few months or a few years, just as they played at general arrangements to borrow, swaps, Roosa bonds, and increased quotas in the International Monetary Fund. But the countries that are adversely affected will rapidly become aware of the injustices and dangers of this new expedient. I hope that first they will endeavor to limit its application as much as possible, and that very soon they will be convinced that another remedy must be found.

### 3. GOLD

The possibility of being reimbursed for dollar and sterling balances with special drawing rights can only satisfy those holding such balances during a short initial period. Afterward they will surely be unwilling to hang on to these balances voluntarily or to increase them. The term "balances" is used here in the broad sense, which includes all attendant ills: the Roosa bonds, swaps, quotas in the International Moneary Fund, and above all, Eurodollars.

In other words, convertibility of these monetary assets into special drawing rights will fail to slow the quest for tangible goods, or perhaps will spur it on faster, along with the concomitant rush to get rid of assets denominated in money.

As long as this preference for real wealth goes on, the deterioration of the world economic system and especially the rise in interest rates will gather momentum.

To prevent this, there is only one solution: give holders of claims denominated in currency an assurance that they can exchange their claims, if they so wish, for a real asset with stable enough average purchasing power to acquire any other market goods at prices varying only within narrow limits.

The real asset that can be accepted and therefore desired as a medium of exchange can only be gold. There can be no substitute under present conditions, essentially because its production cost is very real, unlike that of purely fiduciary standards, which means that it cannot be created at the discretion of the monetary authorities.

I am not saying, however, that restoration of the gold standard implies the elimination of all forms of nonmetallic money, such as bank notes or bank credit based on the monetization of claims. Nor does it actually require effective circulation of gold specie. The only *sine qua non* for the gold standard's existence is that all forms of money should be convertible into metal, directly or indirectly— even with a floor provision, if metal can only be supplied in bars, but in any case, at a level of equivalence determined once and for all and defining the legal parity of the currency.

The price of gold is immutable under such a system. By contrast, when convertibility of the monetary standard into gold is not assured—as is the case now with the dollar—the price of gold can vary. It increases in particular when the buying power of money declines.

As soon as holders of claims denominated in money are assured that they can again exchange them for a fixed weight of metal, on demand and at sight, *de jure* and *de facto,* it goes without saying that they will cease to desire, and therefore to ask for, conversion. Then and only then the pursuit of tangible wealth and the rise in interest rates will end.

It is hardly rational, people will say, to seek an option to exchange that will no longer be taken advantage of the moment it has been secured. Assuredly, in a world where common sense and authority prevailed unchallenged, holding interest-bearing fiduciary claims would certainly seem more rational than maintaining gold holdings or currency holdings convertible into gold at a fixed rate. But at present the least one can say is that users of money are justified in doubting that the buying power of the currency units in which their fiduciary holdings are denominated is secure, especially when one considers the management line followed by central banks and the policy applied or recommended by international monetary authorities.

Furthermore, in the realm of monetary psychology, things are just the way they are and are not changed easily.

Under present conditions, if we want to end decisively the gradual disruption of the international monetary system, there is only one solution that is of immediate applicability and undoubted efficacy: assure owners of monetary holdings that they can exchange them if they wish to do so some day, for a weight of gold fixed once and for all.

The whole problem, therefore, is to make it feasible again to reimburse in gold the claims denominated in money that have been accumulating under various names and forms.

## THE ONLY SOLUTION

Unfortunately, such a possibility cannot be entertained considering the low nominal value of existing gold stocks. Accumulated indebtedness has created a bankruptcy situation in the monetary sphere. When such a situation exists, it is futile to carp about the past and waste one's efforts in the quest of a solvency that is no longer attainable.

The only realistic thing to do is to divide existing assets among creditors in proportion to the unconsolidated claims that may be presented for reimbursement.

The solution is to increase the price of gold.

This seems all the more natural and justified since the gold price was fixed at its present level in 1934 by President Roosevelt. Since then, all prices in the United States have more than doubled.

In the light of these facts, it appears that dollar balances and all related modalities have merely been a substitute for the increase in nominal value that gold stocks would have undergone, if their value had been reckoned at a price related to other market prices.

Champions of the gold standard will point out that stability of gold parity is the main feature of the system and that if it is modified, as in 1934, the belief will spread that it could be modified again in the future. That could maintain the present uncertainty about the monetary future, with all its adverse effects, especially in the field of interest rates.

But such fears would be totally unjustified. A change in monetary parity is not decided at the time of its introduction but at the time of the disturbances that make it inevitable. The parity change envisaged here is only intended to correct once and for all, as in 1934, the effects of a world war and a long period with the gold-exchange standard. As long as the gold standard operates on a day-to-day basis, the smooth and steady increase in the monetary reserves arising out of the regulating phenomena that it generates maintains the balance between monetary requirements and availabilities. No need for parity changes is to be feared.

Some find it odd that gold should be restored to its rightful place in the hierarchy of prices. Would it be odd to correct a price level as a result of which, because all other prices have risen except the price of gold, the weight of gold accruing to any producer of one ton of steel or coal is more than twice the weight that would have accrued in 1934?

Annual production of gold is reduced in nominal value as well as in weight because its price is unrelated to other market prices. Is it surprising then that output is insufficient relative to the needs arising from economic growth and trade expansion?

Think how wheat output would have fallen if wheat still sold at its 1934 price.

Some people wax indignant about increasing the value of a resource produced by the USSR. But the Soviet Union does not export gold alone. It also exports coal, petroleum, and cotton. Do we want also to keep the prices of those commodities at their 1934 level, in order to reduce the USSR's trading capacity?

Others balk at adding value to the output of South Africa. Yet these are generally the same people that dread a shortage of the metal. Is it realistic to want more of it, and yet to pay less?

Certain persons feign indignation over the unearned profits that would accrue to holders of the yellow metal. Yet the profit from doubling the gold price, minus in many instances prolonged loss of interest for those who hold the metal, hardly compares with the rise in value over the last twenty years of land, buildings, and certain corporate stocks. It is hypocritical to tolerate these profits while objecting to a profit on gold.

For these reasons, I remain convinced that when the futility, or in any case the inefficacy, of special drawing rights has been recognized, we shall resort to the only solution that is simple, practical, and well proven—increasing the price of gold.

## NEED FOR AN INTERNATIONAL CONVENTION

To put this into effect, an international convention is needed. It should include the following commitments:

a. At a certain date, a raise in the price at which the signatory states buy and sell gold, either directly or in terms of dollars.

b. A solemn confirmation that all holders of balances denominated in money—dollar balances, sterling balances, or, if the case arises, franc balances—can, if they so desire, be reimbursed at sight for their claims, either in gold or in foreign exchange at the new parity.

c. An offer to extend gold loans from countries holding gold and having no balances to repay to countries whose metallic reserves are inadequate to meet possible requests for reimbursement even after revaluation. These loans would be financed out of the increased nominal value of their gold holdings resulting from the change in par value.

d. An undertaking by participating countries—in order to avoid a new accumulation of currency balances—not to issue money in the future unless backed by assets in gold or in the national currency. Thus, money would not be issued against foreign-exchange holdings. Such a commitment would simply spell a return to the system prevailing prior to the advent of the gold-exchange standard.

I am convinced that such a convention can be negotiated. It would fit directly into the traditional procedures for cooperation among central banks.

In addition, it would work immediately, I am sure. It would lower interest rates greatly and lastingly, and hence it would generate a considerable increase in investment and a marked growth of employment. Nobody should doubt that these results would not only sweep away the black clouds that block our horizon, but also stir up throughout the world an immense wave of prosperity that would last for a long time.

If any doubts remain, it should suffice to invoke the authority of John Maynard Keynes, who wrote in the *Commercial Manchester Guardian* (Reconstruction Supplement) on 20 April 1922, at a time when he had not yet become Lord Keynes: "If the gold standard could be reintroduced in all of Europe, we all believe that the reform would promote trade and production like nothing else, but also stimulate international credit and transfers of capital to the places where they are most useful. One of the greatest elements of uncertainty would be suppressed."

Sentimental and irrational arguments are the only obstacle at present to adopting the solution desired at the time by Keynes. At any rate, these arguments will be swept away by the disturbances, disorders, and sufferings that Western civilization will undergo if nothing is done to save it.

I earnestly hope that the governments of Western countries will not wait for the ultimate consequence of the present chain of events before making their decision. Before a new tempest breaks out, they should calmly adopt not the palliatives that have been discussed up to now, but the sensible, simple, practical, and proven solution that will give peoples everywhere renewed confidence in their future security, and all the well-being that can and should be procured by technological progress and the growth of investment.

May we act before it is too late.

# XVII

## PRECARIOUS DOMINANCE
## OF THE DOLLAR[1]

### 1. THE MUTATION OF 17 MARCH 1968

People often ask me if the decline in the price of gold has made me change my opinion. I want to state clearly that there is no reason for me to doubt the validity of my previous diagnosis, or of the remedies that I prescribed.

The trouble that I denounced in 1961 has brought about all the consequences I had foreseen: a perennial deficit in America's balance of payments, inflation in creditor countries, and in the end, disruption of the monetary system by requests for reimbursement of the dollar balances so imprudently accumulated.

It was precisely the obvious nature of this disruption that triggered off a profound modification of the international monetary system in March 1968, through a series of measures which, as will be shown presently, are of doubtful effectiveness and will, at best, operate only for a certain time.

The lines that follow will demonstrate the need to restore a durable, efficacious monetary system in the Western world and indicate how this reform can be brought about.

---

[1] Text published in *Le Monde* of 13, 14, and 15 February 1970.

Before going into this, however, I must emphasize that this is by no means an anti-American libel. I like and admire the United States more than anybody else. But I feel sad when I see this great republic imposing upon the world a monetary system that has already caused very serious deterioration in the Western world and that will, if it continues, destroy the very civilization that those who initiated the system claim they are protecting.

## A Matter of Civilization

A convertible currency is one that can be exchanged freely and unreservedly for any other convertible currency of equal value.

The layman often views convertibility as a mere financial technicality. But in reality it is a matter of civilization, for it determines the status of Man.

Here is an edifying example: Until 1958, the franc along with several other currencies on the European Continent was largely inconvertible. No purchases could be made abroad unless payment was duly authorized. Imports were subject to quantitative restrictions. Travel abroad and subscriptions to foreign newspapers or the purchase of foreign books were subject to licensing.

The reforms of late December 1958 and subsequent identical steps restored the convertibility of the French franc, first as regards nonresidents and eventually in respect of the whole population, so that the French were free again to determine in what currency areas they would spend their money—hence where they would travel—and to what use they would put their savings.

Thus convertibility is sought because it confers freedom of choice, not just for reasons of economic orthodoxy or financial esthetics. Convertibility is the indispensable prerequisite to economic freedom.

Currency is a contingent and arbitrary institution. It is always issued or withdrawn by one or several banks as against purchase or sale of assets of equal value. If the substratum or substrata of assets are common to several currency areas, then money can circulate freely between them.

Before 17 March 1968, in all Western countries money was issued against gold, against claims denominated in the national currency, or against claims denominated in foreign currencies payable in gold—that is, in fact, against dollars. This system was called the gold-exchange standard.

Of course, American citizens were not authorized to claim reimbursement in gold of their dollar holdings. But every dollar surrendered to a foreign bank of issue and presented by the latter to the American authorities for reimbursement was exchanged for an equivalent amount of gold.

Furthermore, each dollar could be sold freely in the London gold market, where the banks of issue that had formed the gold pool (50 percent of the gold requirement being met by the United States and 50 percent by the other members) supplied whatever amount of gold was demanded, at the official parity of one ounce of gold for $35.

With the operation of this double outlet, anybody holding dollars was certain that he could obtain at any time, without any justification or controls, the quantity of gold representing the amount of money that he held. By moving that gold to any land he chose, he could freely obtain any currency he wished.

Thus the existing monetary system was one of two-tier convertibility: convertibility into dollars, based, in respect of or through the dollar, on convertibility into gold. Of course money users did not notice this mechanism, but through exchange brokers' and arbitragers' transactions, it operated silently and with great precision.

Under this complex system, monetary convertibility was fully assured and guaranteed in all circumstances.

THE EXPLOSION OF MARCH 1968

It has often been said that the gold-exchange standard ought to be replaced because it had ceased to operate. In fact, it operated too easily. That is why it blew up on 17 March 1968.

Indeed, what happened on that day showed that the dollar was truly and unrestrictedly convertible.

The gold-exchange standard made it possible to accumulate dollars beyond all prudence in creditor countries. As I had foreseen and warned as early as 1961, these countries got tired of having to accept indefinitely growing amounts of U.S. currency which were totally useless to them, considering that the United States was running a balance-of-payments deficit.

Eventually, these countries decided—as they were entitled to do and as they would have been under the obligation to do from day to day under the gold standard—to claim reimbursement in gold of substantial proportions of their dollar balances, so that they could obtain marks, Swiss francs, French francs, or even gold bars.

Thus the United States alone had already lost $771 million worth of gold in November and December 1967. On 12 March 1968, $450 million worth of yellow metal had also been moved from Fort Knox to feed the gold pool. On 14 March, in London and Paris, the gold rush took on "phenomenal proportions," as one commentator put it. That evening, the U.S. Government asked the British authorities to close down the London gold market. On Sunday, 17 March 1968, the members of the gold pool decided to terminate operations, which had become too costly.

They were then faced with two alternatives: to remedy the causes of the gold fever by resorting to the kind of medicine that I had unceasingly advised, or else totally to disrupt the temperature-regulating device, by bringing about a situation involving controls and thereby severe limitations on the possibility for non-U.S. holders of dollars to convert them into gold or any other currency they chose.

The latter course was adopted and became effective, as a full range of measures were hastily enacted in Washington on 17 March 1968.

### The Decisions of 17 March

In their communiqué issued after the conference, the governors of the central banks of Belgium, Italy, the Netherlands, Switzerland, the United Kingdom, and the United States noted that the U.S. Government would continue buying and selling gold at the existing price of $35 an ounce, but *only in transactions with monetary authorities.* This meant that as far as the U.S. Government was concerned, gold would not be bought from or sold to private persons or nonmonetary public agencies.

The six governors decided that from then on, official gold holdings should be used solely for transfers between monetary authorities and that they would therefore cease to supply gold to the London and other markets. This clearly implied that the gold pool was being terminated.

Lastly, as they felt that the existing gold stock was fully adequate in view of the forthcoming creation of special drawing rights, they decided that they would no longer buy gold in any market whatsoever or sell any to monetary authorities to replace any amount that they might have sold in private markets.

However, since 1 January 1970, due to the fact that the price of gold in the free market has reverted to a level approximating its official par value, an agreement between the United States and South Africa and approved by the Board of Governors of the International Monetary Fund, authorizes the IMF, notwithstanding the above decision, to buy limited quantities of gold from South Africa under strictly defined conditions. This agreement has not been published in full, but it would seem that it authorizes South Africa to sell gold to the IMF whenever the gold price in London is less than $35 an ounce "on condition that the daily sale amounts only to one-fifth of the weekly amount South Africa must sell to keep its balance of payments in equilibrium."

Starting on 1 January 1970, the stock of international liquidities was supplemented by the creation of "special drawing rights" allocated annually to member countries of the IMF in proportion to their quotas in the fund. The amount permitted to be issued was set at $9.5 billion over a period of three years, including $3.5 billion during the first year. This rule will allow the United States $867 million for 1970.

## Be Careful, Someone Is Watching You

At first, the decisions of 17 March were seen as mere expedients intended to cope with temporary difficulties.

In fact, they add up to a very refined and orderly mechanism that operates to close all avenues for converting dollars into other currency or gold, except the one that runs through the U.S. authorities, who are thus in a position to control requests for such conversion.

The effect of the March decisions is to plug all channels through which the gold market could be fed from official sources.

The stock of monetary gold has been set irrevocably at the level existing on 17 March 1968, subject to the very limited purchases from South Africa, which, as was explained above, have been authorized as from 1 January 1970.

Assuredly, gold can circulate between banks of issue. Its role is that of a pile of chips that move from one gambler to another but whose total may not be increased.

On the other hand, newly mined gold may be sold only to buyers who are not the monetary authorities, except for the small amounts authorized from South Africa. Thus the decisions of 17 March imply the emergence of a free gold market where the monetary authorities are precluded from offering to buy or to sell gold. In the absence of any demand by the monetary authorities, the price of gold should normally decline to the point where there will be huge private purchases or (when the price falls to $35 an ounce, or below) direct limited purchases by the IMF.

From now on, the central banks will no longer be able to buy gold in the London or in any other market. They will therefore no longer be able to convert dollars into gold at the official price, or to convert the dollars held by them or sold to them by private holders, unless they apply specifically to the U.S. monetary authorities, and to them alone.

Thus the ultimate goal and underlying reason of the reforms of 17 March 1968 become clear. Their purpose is to force anybody seeking to convert dollars into gold to go through the narrow channel of some U.S. monetary authority, thereby making the request for conversion obvious and conspicuous. The steps taken enable the American authorities to watch with alertness and exert "friendly" pressure on non-American monetary officials, so that they will refrain from requesting conversion operations that they would like to effect. In other words, so that they will agree to hold on to the dollars that they were tempted to get rid of, and while keeping them, invest them in the U.S. market.

This kind of control was not feasible as long as the London and related gold markets existed. From now on, such panicky unloadings of dollars as occurred in the early part of 1968 will be impossible to the extent—but only to the extent—that the pressure exerted by the U.S. authorities on non-U.S. monetary authorities holding dollars remains effective. The dollar will have become an inconvertible currency for all countries that are under U.S. influence because they need American military protection (like Germany) or want U.S. friendship for political reasons or depend on the United States economically.

## Dollar Convertibility

To the extent that dollar balances outside the United States can no longer be converted into gold, the substratum of all convertible currencies is no longer gold but the dollar.

Under the new system, any holder of dollars wishing to exchange them for some other currency will refrain from requesting the United States to supply gold, as he would be entitled to do in principle under the decisions of 17 March. He will exchange dollars for the currency he desires in an exchange market. The monetary authorities of the country whose currency he desires, if they are to keep the exchange value of their currency from appreciating above the official parity, will be required by the provisions of the Bretton Woods IMF agreement, Article VIII, Section 4, to buy dollars that are offered, and pay for them with an amount of their national currency of equal value.

But in practice, these dollars cannot be exchanged for gold because of the moral pressure exerted by the U.S. Government. The country whose money has been purchased with dollars will have to keep them. The best that can be done to keep these dollars from being too conspicuous is to place them in the Eurodollar market on a short-term or medium-term basis.

The accuracy of this analysis has been verified during the waves of speculation on the mark in the fall of 1968 and spring of 1969. Dollars with which marks were purchased were not exchanged for gold; instead, they swelled by a corresponding amount, albeit temporarily, the dollar balance held by Germany.

From the legal point of view, the difference between the system prior to 17 March 1968 and the system that followed appears slight. But in fact, it has huge repercussions. Under the former system, dollar balances were retained only by those monetary authorities that wanted to. Under the present system, their conversion into gold is practically impossible for countries that are the friends of the United States or seek U.S. friendship.

Under such a system, convertibility is no longer based on gold, but on the dollar.

The consequences of this modification showed immediately in the variations of the U.S. gold stock. It was declining at a fast rate before 17 March, whereas dollar balances were only growing slowly. After 17 March, not only did the U.S. gold stock stop shrinking, but it trended upward. At the same time, dollar balances held by foreigners were growing at an accelerated pace, as were investments in the Eurodollar market.

Thus, the agreements of 17 March brought about a change of considerable scope in the structure of the international monetary system, which has remained legally the gold-exchange standard but has to all intents and purposes become a dollar standard. The *de facto* situation is very close to that which would have existed legally if the United States had promulgated a gold embargo.

## 2. A PRECARIOUS TYPE OF CONVERTIBILITY

As shown by the foregoing analysis, the dollar has remained theoretically convertible into gold or foreign currencies since 17 March 1968. But the system is one of "convertibility under surveillance."

What would happen if residual requests for conversion of dollars into foreign exchange or gold in excess of offsetting operations in exchange markets were more than the United States could satisfy? Clearly, the only conversion window still open—i.e., the one run by the American monetary authorities—would have to be closed.[2] This would mean an embargo on gold by the United States, and a free market would develop where the dollar could be exchanged for foreign currencies at prices below official parities.

Such a situation would be so grave for the whole Western world that it behooves us to assess the inherent dangers.

### CONVERTIBLE ONLY AS LONG AS YOU DON'T CONVERT

To meet possible requests for conversion of dollars into other currencies or gold, the following devices are available to the United States:

—An allocation of special drawing rights totalling $867 million for the current year.

—Ordinary drawing rights on the International Monetary Fund. These can be estimated at about $1,033 million for the "super gold tranche," which can be used unconditionally, plus about $6,450 million for those gold "tranches" that can be used under various conditions.

—A gold stock worth about $11 billion. But, for reasons of national defense, there is little likelihood that the U.S. Government would allow this last reserve of purchasing power abroad to shrink below a certain minimum that is probably close to the present level.

2 That happened on 15 August 1971.

On the other side of the ledger, demand liabilities, denominated in gold or foreign exchange, are quite substantial and consist mainly of dollar balances held by foreigners—banks of issue, international and regional organizations, banks or banking establishments and corporations with headquarters outside the United States, and finally private individuals, including U.S. citizens residing abroad.

The amount of these balances is estimated to be about $42 billion (in the *Federal Reserve Board Bulletin* of November 1969).

But the existence of Eurodollar liabilities considerably increased this negative balance. Total claims denominated in Eurodollars are evaluated at $30 billion dollars by Milton Friedman.[3] However, these liabilities in Eurodollars do not augment U.S. foreign indebtedness by their full amount. A sizable portion of this amount in Eurodollars, perhaps one-fourth or one-third, is covered by liquidities held in the United States by debtor foreign banks. If Eurodollar claims were surrendered by their holders to their respective central banks, U.S. foreign liabilities would be increased by the full part of such claims that is not matched by dollar balances already included in the above total.

It would therefore be useless to attempt to determine with any degree of precision the aggregate amount of liquid claims that encumber U.S. liquidities. But we can be certain that they are far in excess of the amount of resources available to meet them.

One might point out that this is the situation of all banking establishments, whose liquidities are never more than a small fraction of their liabilities.

This comparison, however, is not justified. For financial institutions can always discount with their central bank the whole or part of the short- and medium-term claims in their hands. On the contrary, the United States could not, if the need arose, secure additional cash resources to meet a mass inflow of requests for conversion of dollars into other currencies or gold unless their

---

[3] *The Morgan Guaranty Survey* of October 1969, p. 4.

balance of payments ran a surplus, which is not the case at present and, *ceteris paribus,* appears unlikely in the near future.

One can admit that under current conditions a mass inflow of requests for conversion of dollars into gold like the one in March 1968 could not be met out of official U.S. liquidities abroad.

This leads to the conclusion that dollar convertibility will be maintained and a gold embargo avoided only insofar as countries other than the United States agree to increase their dollar balances and refrain from requesting conversion into nondollar currencies or gold of the balances that they hold or have further acquired by virtue of their agreement.

This accounts for the efforts undertaken by the U.S. Government, with all the powerful means of pressure at its disposal, to get holders of dollar balances to abstain from requesting conversion.

Obviously, the disappearance of any gold market operating at the official rate was a prerequisite if such pressures were to be effective. By compelling foreign holders of dollars to go through the U.S. monetary authorities, they gave the latter an opportunity to tell anybody wishing to shed his load of dollars: "Be good; we are watching you."

## How Long Will the Sheep Follow?

As long as non-American holders of dollars stay "good," dollar convertibility into gold and foreign exchange will certainly be maintained. And the Bretton Woods system, supplemented by the decisions of 17 March 1968, will survive. But will they always "behave"?

Some forty years ago, a Belgian banker emerged very disgruntled from a stormy stockholders' meeting and vented his feelings in the following words: "When things go well, they are sheep. When business is bad, they are lions. But," he added arrogantly, "they always behave like animals."

I shall not adopt his final comparison, which is unduly insulting. But I must note that as long as "things go well," governments and private individuals or entities holding dollar balances or Euro-dollars will yield to U.S. pressure and agree to keep the dollars, as well as those that have further accrued to them as a result of the U.S. balance-of-payments deficit.

This can go on for a long time. But it seems to me impossible that, as time goes by, unforeseeable events such as the continuation of the U.S. balance-of-payments deficit, a deterioration of the economic situation, or even some banking or financial incident, a shift in the balance of power, a possible reversal of some alliances, or simply the evolution of thought and feeling, should not affect the subservience of dollar holders and induce them to request conversion of their dollar holdings in whole or in part, even at the risk of antagonizing the Washington authorities.

a. A primary source of growing tension would be continued growth of dollar balances, resulting from a continued deficit in the U.S. balance of payments. Piling up dollars cannot but make people allergic to them eventually.

Now, I have often shown that accumulating dollar balances, whether invested in U.S. bank deposits and treasury bills, or in the European markets in the form of Eurodollars loanable to U.S. borrowers, enabled the American economy as a whole to immediately retrieve payments made abroad to settle its balance-of-payments deficit.

Thus, the mechanics of the accumulation of dollar balances make the U.S. balance-of-payments deficit possible and tend to perpetuate it. Until now, experience has always confirmed this affirmation, notwithstanding predictions to the contrary by the highest U.S. authorities.

b. Creditor countries cannot fail to realize one day that through the accumulation of dollar balances they are the ones who pay for the tangible assets acquired in their own territory by U.S. citizens or corporations, at least so long as they cannot secure repatriation of their holdings invested in the United States. Thus the United States is buying factories, businesses, and corporations, and even financing some of its foreign aid and prestige expenditures at the expense of these creditor countries.

It is unthinkable that the United States, a proud and generous nation, will not in the end be disgusted by practices that permit it to live at the expense of its suppliers and the recipients of its aid. I am convinced that if this goes on, Westerners will finally open their eyes, become aware of the effects of an unprecedented system of spoliation, and demand that an end be put to it.

c. Prolonged accumulation of dollar balances by certain creditor countries strengthens their national currencies by increasing their foreign-exchange reserves. This tends to induce speculative purchases of these currencies, while eliminating influences that inhibit or restrain the scope of such speculation.

The recent events that have affected the mark—in conjunction, of course, with prospects of a devaluation of the franc and a revaluation of the deutschmark—afford a decisive example of this perverse effect. For example, on 15 November 1968, Germany received $800 million. Between 22 April and 9 May 1969, another $4.5 billion entered its bank vaults, followed by $1.9 billion from 1 to 29 September. Germany was morally bound to hold on to these additional dollar balances; otherwise it would have requested the United States—as was its right, under the commitments of 17 March 1968, and its duty toward its own citizens— to pay gold for the dollars it had acquired. Such reimbursement would have reduced the U.S. gold reserves by a corresponding amount, causing in the United States a credit shrinkage that would immediately have halted speculation on revaluation of the mark by drying up purchasing power.

d. Furthermore, reducing the U.S. gold reserves would have forced the government to put an embargo on gold, in other words, to devalue its currency sooner or later. But instead, Germany had to agree to revalue its own currency to check the inflow of foreign liquidities, because it could not restrain speculation by giving a real content to the transfers of capital that resulted. Thus Germany shouldered the economic consequences of a speculative tide for which it was in no way responsible.

As long as the dollar-balance-retention dogma is maintained, the United States will be protected against any danger of devaluation. When its balance of payments runs a deficit, the creditor country or countries will have to revaluate.

Can one possibly imagine that the peoples of the world will agree indefinitely to a situation whereby the United States would be the only nation in the world that would not need to worry about balance-of-payments problems?

I wrote in 1961 that the retention of dollar balances by creditor countries conferred upon the United States the secret of running "deficits without tears." The unquestionable efficiency of this secret was verified during the crisis of the deutschmark.

e. Naturally the U.S. authorities can try to bring about the credit shrinkages that would have resulted from reimbursement of the dollar balances arising out of the deficit. That is what they are doing now.[4]

But whereas the operation of the gold standard would have forced the necessary adjustments from day to day—that is to say, imperceptibly—the need to abruptly correct the cumulative effects of a protracted period of inaction leads to a bout of really fierce deflation.

Such a course implies dangers of recession and unemployment, not only for the United States, but for all countries in the dollar area, as will become increasingly apparent.

Can one really imagine that sovereign states will indefinitely allow the course of their economies to be determined by a policy that is entirely beyond their control and from which they derive no profit except inflation inside their own boundaries?

One day they will wake up. Then they will rebel, and demand that an end be put to the accumulation of dollar balances, which is the root of all evil.

f. The obligation of keeping dollar balances creates a state of dependence that is not only economic but also political. What freedom of choice does a country have when its monetary reserves—which are the instrument of and the prerequisite for the convertibility of its currency—are deposited abroad? In some cases, like Germany's or Japan's, this dependence can be willingly accepted

[4] In February 1970.

in exchange for military guarantees or economic outlets that the countries concerned consider essential. But can we expect such circumstances to continue indefinitely? When they cease, resistance against the existing system is bound to assume considerable proportions and to destroy it.

g. Everybody knows that a total disruption of the system will eventually entail a rise in the price of gold, notwithstanding reassuring words to the contrary. Countries whose convertibility reserves consist of dollars rather than metal will be deprived of the incremental value that would have resulted from the holding of an equal amount of gold.

Who can doubt that the monetary officials of those countries will one day realize that their duty is to safeguard the interests of the citizens who entrusted them with office at least as much and even more than those of the United States? On that day they will seek to reduce their dollar balances—as one of the most deeply committed countries in the Far East is already doing—or in any event will refuse to increase such balances.

For the reasons listed above, the indefinite retention of dollar balances will one day cease to be a respected principle. The convertibility of the dollar will no longer be assured, and the monetary system will then collapse.[5]

One hardly dares imagine the ensuing damage and turmoil. The least that is to be feared is that most of the affected countries will be forced to protect their balances of payments with all the isolationist economic practices that blossomed so harmfully in 1931–1935. The inevitable result would be recession and unemployment. Additional dangers will result, compounded by the weakness of political structures that are far less solid than at the time of the Great Depression.

It is not possible for Western countries to assume such risks just to preserve the myth of the convertibility of the dollar, which is maintained only through the temporary expedient of the retention of dollar balances, imposed from outside. It is inconceivable that the United States, conscious as it is of its responsibilites, should use

[5] This happened on 15 August 1971.

the influence resulting from its power to continue imposing this myth upon the world.

If Western civilization is to be saved, the danger must be removed coolly and deliberately before an explosion occurs.

Remedies exist. They are simple and proven.

### 3. WAYS TO RESTORE ENDURING CONVERTIBILITY

It is clear that the dollar standard is vulnerable because its outcome is a huge accumulation of dollar balances. These, by reason of their cumulative growth resulting from America's balance-of-payments deficit, cannot but induce circumstances that one day will lead those who held them to try to get rid of them.

When that day comes, the survival of convertibility will depend on the efficiency of the "friendly" pressure that obliges countries holding dollar balances to keep them. Of course it is only legitimate that banking systems, and central banks in particular, should keep large amounts of dollars and other currencies for day-to-day settlements. But if their retention is to last for any length of time, such holdings must be viewed as necessary by their owners, in view of their forseeable cash requirements or for reasons of convenience. Otherwise, they can only be persuaded to keep them if they are offered high interest rates, which, like those obtaining at present, can only in the long run hamper the large investments needed for economic growth and social welfare.

Even so, it is by no means certain—considering the interdependence of markets—that the process of gradual equalization of interest rates will not impair or nullify the protection resulting for the debtor country from high interest rates.

Convertibility of the currencies of the Western world, which is largely based on the assertion that dollar balances are in fact convertible, can only be maintained if these balances are brought down to a level where the country holding them can never regard them as undesired.

To achieve this, there are two solutions, and two only: first, to consolidate or reimburse that part of the dollar balances which is clearly in excess of foreseeable needs, and is retained only because of submission to U.S. pressure; and second, to prevent the growth of new balances.

## How to Consolidate or Reimburse the Volatile Portion of Dollar Balances

The contractual consolidation of the whole or part of the dollar balances that might become unwanted would remove to a corresponding degree the danger of mass requests for reimbursement.

This method was successfully followed by Britain for a considerable part of the sterling balances that threatened the pound's convertibility.

But this solution can only be applied within narrow limits. For dollar balances in the countries holding them are the counterpart of a proportion of the currency in circulation that is often substantial, and are considered a part of the liquidities needed for payments that might be requested in foreign currencies.

The only solution for the portion of the dollar balances that cannot be consolidated would be to reimburse them in gold or international liquidities. This solution would be all the more legitimate since the agreement of 17 March 1968 expressly provided for and confirmed the feasibility of such an outcome.

Yet reimbursement by the U.S. Government of an important fraction of existing dollar balances would undoubtedly reduce its reserves of gold and international liquidities to nothing. Such a solution is simply unthinkable. Therefore, other resources are required to effect such reimbursements as are regarded as absolutely necessary.

In practice, these resources cannot be procured without a process of deflation that would kill economic growth, short of a rise in the price of gold.

I regret I have to come to this finding here. For I realize that it will be irksome to many readers, and will estrange some who consider raising the gold price to be abnormal and cheap.

But the problem is to find at once resources far in excess of the annual saving capacity.

Furthermore, increasing the price of gold cannot be viewed as illegitimate, considering that dollar balances have simply replaced in the cash holdings of the banks of issue the increment in nominal value that they would have derived from their—and in particular the U.S.—gold stock, had the gold price risen along with other prices. Using such increments to reimbuse dollar balances would be simply replacing a precarious possession with the metallic asset that it imperfectly represents.

As for the criticism leveled on moral grounds at the idea of re-valuing gold stocks, I think that I have discussed and for the most part refuted this in previous chapters.[6] I will not go into this again except to recall that the value increment that would result from doubling the price of gold stocks would be much smaller than the increments that have accrued to owners of land, buildings, and securities as a result of price increases in which only stocks of monetary gold have not been allowed to participate.

As to the margin by which the price of gold might be raised, that can only be determined after a comprehensive study, taking into account all the facts of the case and in particular the amount of those balances that cannot be consolidated amicably, as well as the decline in the average cost of mining gold due to technological progress. The greater the portion of dollar balances that can be consolidated on an amicable basis, the lower the price increase in gold that will be necessary.

At any rate, pegging up the gold price will make it possible to replace a major part of the unconsolidated balances by gold hold-ings of equal value.

In this connection, I wish to make it clear once again, to avoid a frequent misunderstanding, that I would consider it a crime against economic stability to raise the price of gold without using the value increment to reimburse dollar balances.

Yet some special cases will need to be dealt with. First of all,

---

6 In particular in "What Is to Be Will Be," pages 175–176.

Britain, which has little gold and sizable sterling balances. It would seem that an appreciable portion of these balances has not yet been consolidated, although figures to confirm this are not available.

The resources needed for the reimbursement of those balances that the British Government considers expedient to reimburse—if any, and, if so, those alone—should be made available to it in the form of soft loans arising out of levies on the increased nominal value of the gold stocks of countries that have no balances to reimburse.

Another part of the increased value of the gold stocks of these same countries could also be used to finance long-term loans to reinforce the gold reserves of countries that did not have enough metal to participate in a system of restored convertibility.

That such convertibility would be of a continuing nature, because resumption of settlements in gold would restore balances of payments to equilibrium, is borne out by so many precedents that any demonstration would be otiose. Those who entertain any doubt on this point should refer to my previous statements.[7] Some criticisms of these expositions appeared to me to be so inapposite that they tended to confirm my findings rather than casting doubt on their validity.

However that may be, restoring enduring convertibility requires international commitments undertaken simultaneously and strictly adhered to.

I have had occasion to specify the provisions that such an international convention should include.[8] May I merely recall here that the convention should comprise an undertaking not to increase existing dollar and sterling balances after a certain date; to increase the price of gold, as expressed in the various national currencies, at the same date and by an equal proportion everywhere; in the case of the United States and Britain, to use the resulting supplemental value of their gold stocks to reimburse their dollar and sterling

[7] Especially *Balance of Payments* (New York: Macmillan, 1967).
[8] In particular in Chapter XVI above.

balances; and for countries holding gold and having no balances to reimburse, to use part of the increased nominal value of their gold reserves for low-interest loans to countries that need to increase their gold holdings to restore the gold-convertibility of their currency.

Evidence that such a convention is feasible is afforded by the precedent of the agreements of 17 March 1968. However, these agreements were adopted in the heat of a veritable gold rush. It is highly unlikely that governments of the main Western countries have sufficient freedom of action or clearsightedness to adopt, except in time of crisis, a solution that is violently opposed by U.S. public opinion and is very unpopular in some other countries.

Yet the considerations adduced in the preceding section of this chapter leave no doubt that one day—which cannot be far away but remains unforeseeable—events will occur that will seriously threaten convertibility of the dollar.[9]

When that day comes, a solution will be urgent. I am certain, alas, that there can be no other than the one I have outlined.

It will foster throughout the world a powerful tide of renewed confidence, financial stability, economic growth, and social progress.

May that solution be adopted before it is too late.

[9] These events occurred on 15 August 1971.

# EPILOGUE

We are reaching the end of this book, but this is not the end of the great adventure whose beginning it recounts.

At the stage of the story that we have reached, one thing is certain: the nations of the West are laboring under a system that is not a *de jure* but a *de facto* system of inconvertibility.[1] The printing-press phenomenon has assumed new modalities, which are called SDR's, swap arrangements, or quota increases in the IMF. But under the protection of monetary inconvertibility, the printing press can meet all market solicitations, with practically no limitations.

It is a fact that the gold-exchange standard is not the only possible source of inflation. Even under a system of gold convertibility, any country can apply a fiscal or monetary policy that generates an excess of aggregate demand over the aggregate value of total supply, thereby running a balance-of-payments deficit. Hence the fact that the perverseness arising out of a system under

[1] This was written in 1970. The inconvertibility is, since 15 August 1971, *de jure*.

which certain foreign currencies are monetized is not a prerequisite to economic disequilibrium, but suffices to bring it on.

Conversely, the monetary authorities of reserve-currency countries—in the present case, the United States—could, in theory, if they followed an adequate credit policy, mop up the liquidity surplus arising out of the feedback to the country of origin of payments made abroad.

But experience shows that this is a purely academic eventuality. Except under a fully totalitarian regime, one cannot possibly imagine that the monetary authorities of a reserve currency country could, by mopping up some purchasing power, bring about a contraction in the money supply of the same magnitude as would have been caused by a balance-of-payments deficit of the same scope, under the gold standard.

If one entertains any doubts in this respect, U.S. experience would suffice to dispel them. Here is a powerful country endowed with the most learned and the most efficient banking institutions, which ostensibly, in the eyes of the whole world, undertakes to restore its balance-of-payments equilibrium, but refuses to resort to the methods of monetary control, which it regards as barbaric and outdated. The distinguished Secretary of the Treasury, Mr. owler, solemnly proclaimed in July 1965 a restoration program and schedule, stating: "The deficit will be reduced by half by the end of 1965 and fully eliminated by the end of 1966." The Secretary had such confidence in the efficacy of his policy that he regarded as essential "the deliberate creation of a new reserve instrument (the special drawing rights) to replace the additional liquidity arising out of the U.S. balance-of-payments deficit, which is not expected to continue."

We know what happened subsequently.

The attempt to bring the external deficit under control without using the monetary instrument was pushed to its extreme limits by the grandiose San Antonio Plan of 1 January 1968.[2] President

---

[2] See page 153 above.

Johnson was endeavoring to restore the balance of external commitments through administrative manipulations in the most varied fields.

This yielded paltry results. The superb indifference of the U.S. balance of payments in response to the forecasts of the all-powerful head of the American Treasury and to the solicitations of the President of the United States, together with its modest and continuing submission to the perverse effects of the gold-exchange standard, should make even the blind see—by showing them the overwhelming nature of monetary influences compared to all other interventions, however powerful these may be.

This negative lesson is supported, *a contrario*, by the events that affected the French balance of payments in 1968. In the face of the mass capital outflows that were taking place, the Central Bank would not take any action and even abstained from raising the discount rate, which remained imperturbably at the level of 3.5 percent until 3 July 1968. Between 2 May and 21 November 1968, 17.7 billion francs left France, while the Central Bank, far from attempting to hold them back by tightening credit, created an additional 23.3 billion francs of credit.

The indifference of a balance of payments—that of the United States—to measures that do not affect credit, and the strict subservience of another balance of payments—that of France—to monetary procedures, throw into full relief the futility of bringing to bear any action of a nonmonetary nature against the balance of international commitments, and *a contrario* the efficacy of procedures based on the regulation of the aggregate volume of credit.

In the face of such lessons, can anyone believe that the International Monetary Fund, the Committee of Ten, or any other multinational authorities can bring about, by way of authoritative decisions, the variations in aggregate demand that gold transfers would have generated, had they been allowed to take place unrestricted? Can anyone believe that such authorities have sufficient power to cause a credit shrinkage of sufficient magnitude to restore the balance? Who could possibly believe that public opinion and governments would accept the dangers of a recession that might result from such measures?

There is a huge difference between the slow, gradual, day-to-day—and therefore hardly perceptible—effect of the variations in purchasing power that result from international settlements and the sudden, massive, and generally tragic impact of contraction measures enacted by the monetary authorities.

Someone has said that the general public would no longer agree to submit to the blind tutelage of the monetary factor. But because it would not, the general public has suffered widespread inflation, a revival of American isolationism, the end of trade liberalization, the first measures of restriction on international financial transactions and, above all, interest rates at a level that prohibits any lasting economic development.

From now on, considering that inconvertibility is the dominant feature of the international monetary system, world equilibrium hinges only on the knowledge, the wisdom, and the independence of the monetary authorities.

Awareness of the results that these qualities have yielded over the last decade, at a time when they had been pushed to an extreme, augurs ill for their future impact.

As long as we do not restore a convertible-currency system, with adjustments to take into account the fact that the gold-exchange standard has perverted the system created at Bretton Woods, the world will be doomed to suffer balance-of-payments disequilibriums, monetary insecurity, migrations of hot money, exchange-rate instability, and all the distempers that the ignorance of men and the weakness of institutions can beget.

When one watches the evolution of the international monetary system, it looks as if the West were bent on putting into practice Lenin's saying that "to destroy bourgeois society, you must debauch its money."[3] How can we allow this kind of mistake to be

[3] Quoted by Joseph Schumpeter, in *Capitalism, Socialism, and Democracy* (New York: Harper & Row, 1950), p. 227.

made by a country that has devoted so much effort and so much care to preserve for itself as well as for others the free-enterprise system, and has shed so much blood in defense of freedom throughout the world?

Let us hope that before it is too late we will entrust again to monetary mechanisms the tasks that the feeble hands and vacillating minds of men are unable in the present circumstances to assume.

# AFTERWORD TO THE AMERICAN EDITION: OCTOBER, 1971

Those wounds heal ill that men do give themselves;
Omission to do what is necessary
Seals a commission to a blank of dangers
—Patroclus in Shakespeare's *Troilus and Cressida*

Even since 1961, public opinion had regarded me as prophesier of evil: one who portended momentous events that no-one believed would happen. Cassandra, they used to call me.

Today, no-one can doubt that Cassandra was right: I had foretold that the international monetary system would inevitably bring about a U.S. balance-of-payments deficit, inflation—first in creditor countries, then in the community of convertible-currency countries—and lastly the dislocation, in an atmosphere of general collapse, of the international monetary system, by reason of the accumulation of sight claims on U.S. gold.

The first two sets of consequences have already come to pass. The third has been unfolding before us since 17 March 1968: the gradual and inexorable destruction of the structure built at Bretton Woods, which came to an end on 15 August 1971.

However, it would be puerile to go on repeating "I told you so." What is important is to note that my prediction was no prophesy but only the expression of a logical necessity that should not have escaped the attention of a conscious observer.

Today the disintegration is obvious, undeniable, and perceptible to anyone.

But public opinion is still being misled and told that the evil is only the consequence of a very slight overevaluation of certain currencies and of the inflation generated in the United States by the inadequacy of the credit policy.

The U.S. balance-of-payments deficit is attributable to a minor extent only to its trade balance, which alone is directly affected by relative prices as resulting from existing exchange parities. The deficit is essentially attributable to capital movements.

That there is inflation in the United States cannot be doubted. But inflation has been existing for a much shorter period of time than the balance-of-payments deficit. Taking account of its present level, U.S. inflation remains substantially less than the inflation that for many years now has beset the main creditor countries.

Of course, erratic price disparities could exist and exchange parity adjustments could temporarily reduce or reverse them, but to the extent that such price modifications would result from a revaluation —that is, the establishment of a new fixed parity—they will allow the major shortcoming of the previous system to continue. By this I mean, the unlimited absorption by the creditor countries of dollars which, as they cannot be converted into gold or foreign exchange, will be immediately reinvested in the United States. After a revaluation operation, the system will still be what it was before: as soon as the respite brought about by exchange parity adjustments has come to an end, the U.S. balance-of-payments deficit will reemerge and persist.

If no revaluation takes place and if the creditor countries only suspend their purchase of dollars on a fixed parity basis, the exchange rate for the dollar, which will have become a floating rate, will result only from the supplies of and demands for dollars in the exchange markets. Can one imagine that holders of fantastic masses of dollar or Eurodollar balances, henceforward without any fixed value in terms of gold or indeed in terms of any non-American currency, will indefinitely abstain from demanding in the exchange market the counterpart in a third currency of their holdings? Their demand, when manifested in the market, will bring about a far-reaching depreciation in dollar rates.

Such depreciation will further disrupt trade flows. It will generate in many countries retaliatory measures against what will thus be wrongly called American dumping. It will give rise to bouts of isolationism likely to result in the most tragic circumstances in the field of international economic and political relations. It will create throughout the world a breeding ground for recession and unemployment. As regards the standard of living of the peoples, it will destroy all that had been gained as a result of trade liberalization.

Can one believe that exisitng political structures, already undermined by those ideologies that thrive on inflation, can long resist such shattering blows?

Anyone really wishing to save the West from an impending catastrophe must first identify the problem to be resolved and then endeavor to find a solution.

## Identification of the Problem

In present conditions, the top priority should go to an attack on the causes that jeopardize stability and endurance.

The problem can be formulated as follows:

1. Inflation, exorbitant interest rates, the increase of claims to the international liquidities of the United States, will not disappear unless the U.S. balance-of-payments deficit itself is eliminated.

2. In nontotalitarian countries, no system of administrative controls makes it possible to bring about equilibrium in an authoritarian manner in the field of external commitments. Furthermore, it must be noted that under a totalitarian system such methods produce their effects only at the cost of reducing international trade to a minimum.

3. This equilibrium, which cannot be generated by administrative action, can only be brought on by influences regulating the amount of currency as a result of international transfers of purchasing power such as would have taken place under the gold standard.

4. The gold-exchange standard nullifies the effect on the reserve

currency country—in the present case, the United States—of transfers effected with a view to the settlement of its deficits.

5. Equilibrium and endurance will be restored in the Western community of nations only if they eliminate the gold-exchange standard and substitute an international monetary system without any reserve currency. That means a system under which no country can create—except to meet its foreseeable settlements—substantial quantities of domestic currency as against claims denominated in the currency of a third country and in particular against dollars.

6. Such a system must exclude any procedure that would generate unearned international liquidity assets such as SDR's or increases in IMF quotas.

7. In practice, the gold standard alone, supported by credit superstructure which in every country constitute its necessary complement, provides a certainty that the two above requiremens shall be met.

8. The obligation to settle in gold uncompensated international trade balances will make it impossible to use to that end the dollar balances held by creditor countries. As a result, this obligation will generate demands for repayment of existing balances, as is already the case. Such demands, if substantial, will cause a far-reaching depreciation of the dollar, which will undermine the stability of the West and threaten the endurance of the order which it expresses.

In conclusion, the deadlock into which the gold-exchange standard has led the Western community of nations must be resolved.

To that end, two sets of measures are essential:

—In the future, the elimination of the right for banks of issue to create domestic currency as against foreign exchange, even payable in gold, if any, which they would not need to use short-term to service their current commitments.

—The consolidation or reimbursement of all that part of the existing dollar balances whose reimbursement might be demanded.

## The denial and disappearance of the remedy

It is for the implementation of this latter requirement that, in the course of the years which followed my first denunciation of the gold-exchange standard in 1961, I had proposed that the price of gold should be doubled.

In particular, I had expounded a program of action in two articles that were published in *Le Monde* and *The Times Business Review* of 27 September 1966. This program was essentially directed toward the elimination of the reserve currency system. But such elimination would have inevitably given rise to demands for the reimbursement of the major part of existing dollar balances.

Now, such reimbursement could not have been effected unless there had been a very high level of international liquidities. And it was in order to try to generate such high levels of international liquidities that I was led to consider the price of gold.

I observed that the price of gold had been fixed by President Roosevelt at $35 per ounce in 1934 and that since then all prices in the United States had more than doubled.

In 1960, the gold holdings of the United States were in an amount of $17,800 million, and the U.S. gold tranche in the International Monetary Fund was $1,600 million, adding up to total reserve assets of $19,400 million. United States indebtedness to official institutions amounted to $11,100 million and the corresponding figure in respect to private creditors was $7,600 million, adding up to $18,700 million.[1]

One could see immediately that a restoration of the gold price in the general price hierarchy that would lead to roughly doubling the price fixed in 1934 by President Roosevelt at $35 per ounce (on that occasion the price was just about doubled) would increase the nominal value of the federal reserves to $38,800 million, from which $18,700 million could have been used so as to allow the full reimbursement in gold of the dollar balances existing at the time. Thereafter, the Federal Reserve System would still have been

[1] Review of the Federal Bank of St. Louis, July 1971.

left with assets representing $22,100 million, that is $700 million more than before the operation.

The above-mentioned settlement would not have affected the liquidity of the Federal Reserve System because the amount of availabilities required to service currency circulation is obviously assessed not in terms of gold but in terms of currency. Furthermore, the claims that the dollar balances represented were not subject to any gold clause and therefore their holders were entitled only to a sum in dollars strictly equivalent to their nominal amount.

The reimbursement of the major part of foreign-held dollar balances would have made it possible to restore overnight and without incurring the slightest risk the principle of payment in gold of the uncompensated balances of the U.S. balance of payments.

Every precedent that can be adduced allows one to assert that, provided only there was no domestic inflation, the resumption of settlements in gold would have restored the equilibrium of the U.S. balance of payments within a short time. Anyone having any doubt in this respect could refer to the examples adduced in my book *Balance of Payments*.[2]

I must even make it clear that this book was written to counter criticism by an American friend of mine. A very high financial authority himself, but he was not convinced that the purchasing-power-transfer mechanism that operated when allowed free play, unaffected by domestic inflation phenomena, could restore balance-of-payments equilibrium, however jeopardized such equilibrium might be, within a short period—say, a few months rather a few years.

This question of the efficacy of the regulating influence of international commitments is of vital importance in relation to the problem under consideration. This principle, which is taught at most universities, has, so to speak, never been accepted by practical operators. They persist in pursuing external-payments equilibrium through administrative controls, such as those established by Presi-

[2] New York; The Macmillan Company, 1967.

dent Johnson in the United States through his San Antonio program on 1 January 1968. History clearly shows that, except under totalitarian regimes, such efforts have never yielded the desired result. Indeed, history shows that the resumption of settlement in gold of uncompensated balances is a necessary if not sufficient requirement for the balance of payments to be in equilibrium, and that, if you want to achieve such equilibrium, you must effectively ensure such resumption.

But in 1971, the situation was quite different from what it had been in 1961 in relation to the possibility of restoring dollar convertibility into gold through the artificial solution of a rise in the gold price.

First, the American economy was laboring under strong inflationary tendencies that had not existed in 1961.

Furthermore, by the end of 1970 the United States gold stock had been reduced to about $11,100 million and total official reserves, including gold, had fallen to $14,500 million. On the other hand, total dollar balances had risen to $23,900 million as regards public institutions and $21,800 million as regards private institutions, adding up to a total of $45,700 million.[3]

To obtain the full amount of non-American claims that would saddle the U.S. reserves, one must add to this total the whole of that fraction of Eurodollars for which there are no counterpart dollar holdings in the balance sheet of the foreign institution that has issued them, whereas such holdings are already included in the above-mentioned external debt figure of the United States.

All the above figures show that, if in 1971 the intention had been to reimburse a major part of the dollar balances and their various modalities through an increase in the price of gold, the price of gold should have been increased at least threefold. Now, a threefold increase in the price of gold would not merely amount to a restoration of the gold price in the general hierarchy of prices but a substantial raising of its level. This would bring about unbearable distortions, a solution which can no longer be entertained.

[3] Review of the Federal Reserve Bank of St. Louis, July 1971, p. 11.

Whereas I had long been a lone voice in the wilderness when I suggested a solution through a pegging up of the gold price, I had the pleasant surprise of finding in the thoroughly official but also thoroughly objective Review of the Federal Bank of St. Louis (July 1971) a statement of views very close to mine:

> Five years ago, when dollar claims held by foreigners were perhaps no more than twice as large as the U.S. gold stock, it was possible to give serious consideration to a doubling of the dollar price of gold (which would double the dollar value of our gold stock) as a means of restoring U.S. ability to meet all dollar claims at a fixed gold price. Now that total foreign official and private liquid dollar claims are more than three times as large as our gold stock . . . the required threefold increase in the price of gold is beyond reasonable probability of adoption.

Thus, the method that I proposed ten years ago, to liquidate the gold-exchange standard and reconstruct an efficacious system of payments, is no longer adequate. No doubt, the price of gold will rise under market influences, but to an extent that is impossible to predict. Such rise may contribute to the solution of the problem but it is not likely to afford a full solution.

Although one must give up the idea of finding all the resources necessary for the reimbursement of dollar balances in their various forms through an increase in the price of gold, one cannot doubt that their nonreimbursable nature due to the amount that they have now reached represents a very serious threat to the continuance of the existing international monetary system.

There is no precedent showing that reimbursement of a non-reimbursable debt has never been requested. As Paul Valéry put it, "There is nothing more constant than the unforeseen." One day, somewhere in the world, there will occur some unforeseen event— political or social disturbances, an armed conflict, an economic depression, bankruptcy (such as the Creditanstalt failure which in

1931 turned the 1929 cyclical recession into the Great Depression), difficulties in the Eurodollar market—which will induce holders of dollar balances to demand conversion into another currency. When that day comes, if the creditor countries are not prepared to supply all the foreign exchange demanded against a further increase in their already overplentiful stocks of dollars, the U.S. currency will undergo a far-reaching depreciation in exchange markets. As indicated above, such depreciation will usher in serious disruptions in international relations and threaten economic depression and unemployment, as was the case during the 1931–1933 period.

Everything possible must be attempted in order to ward off the recurrence of such events. Measures likely to attenuate if not to avoid them may still be available.

First and foremost, there should be an endeavor to consolidate existing dollar balances on an amicable basis. It is probable that, as far as the United States is concerned, as indeed was the case previously with Britain, a major part of the dollar balances in the hands of public institutions can thus be frozen.

As such a measure will not be fully adequate, some will no doubt suggest the possibility of generating the necessary resources to ensure the reimbursements demanded through U.S. balance-of-payments surpluses. I, for one, cannot imagine that such a solution can yield results commensurate with present requirements within the short time available.

If neither a consolidation of the balances nor international trade can yield the necessary resources to meet demands for payments, some will also no doubt think of creating such resources. Reformers who follow in the wake of my friend Professor Triffin will propose recourse to a substitute currency created from scratch and not convertible into gold, of the SDR type. Such currency would have to be issued not on the basis of reasoned allocations equitably apportioned between all members of the International Monetary Fund, but basically in favor of the United States, to equate the amount of reimbursements with which that country would be faced.

Relying on many precedents, I fear that such issuance could unleash throughout the world a new wave of inflation of considerable amplitude, pushing interest rates to unsustainable levels that could not last long. So long as such hesitations and tergiversation continue, dollar rates will be increasingly weaker in exchange markets. The result will be a corresponding increase in the price of gold in terms of dollars.

If action is taken promptly to revalue existing cash holdings of the United States proportionately with such depreciation, the resulting nominal value increment may yield resources that could be utilized toward the reimbursement of the most volatile fractions of dollar balances.

But there are many states that hold gold stocks and have no balances to reimburse. They are the states whose currencies are not reserve currencies. For those states, the rise in the price of gold will substantially increase the nominal level of their gold reserves. And the general interest, from which they cannot be dissociated, will require that they place at the disposal of the United States, in the form of long-term loans at low rates of interest, part of the value increment accruing to their cash holdings. Such loans would be very akin to the feedback operations that have often been proposed, but they would be supported by real transfers rather than last on the phantasms of loans extended under the gold-exchange system.

U.S. credit itself, which remains exceptionally high, would in itself justify such transfers. This will be all the more easily accepted as the resources transferred will be used forthwith for the reimbursement of claims held by the lenders. Very elaborate schedules must specify to the greatest extent possible a standard ratio between loans extended to and reimbursement secured from each country.

If this method of utilization is accepted by a large majority of gold-holding states and its widespread acceptance is sanctioned by an international convention, a rise in the gold price can have no inflationary effects since it will be offset by a corresponding decrease in the dollar balances in the assets of the gold-lending institutions.

I cannot say whether these procedures will make it possible to ward off the crisis that threatens the West, but if they are to have any chance of success they must be developed and implemented in a systematic way, according to the eligible method, before new crises break out.

Unless this is done, we shall be drifting along in confusion, as in 1931–33, toward the liquidation of the gold-exchange standard.

May we be spared the sufferings and collapse which would inevitably attend such a catastrophe.